The Surrender of Silence

The Surrender of Silence
By Ironfoot Jack Neave; edited by Colin Stanley.
First published by Strange Attractor Press in 2018.

Design and layout by Maia Gaffney-Hyde.

ISBN: 978-1907222-658

Strange Attractor Press
BM SAP, London, WC1N 3XX, UK
www.strangeattractor.co.uk

Distributed by the MIT Press, Cambridge, Massachusetts.
And London, England.
Printed and bound in Estonia by Tallinna Raamatutrükikoda.

THE SURRENDER
OF SILENCE

Being the Memoirs of Ironfoot Jack Neave,
King of the Bohemians

Edited by Colin Stanley
Introduction by Phil Baker

ACKNOWLEDGEMENTS

My thanks to the Estate of Colin Wilson (c/o Joy Wilson)
for allowing me to work on this project.

Timothy Whidborne.

The staff of the Manuscripts and Special Collections Department of
the University of Nottingham.

Sue Grimwood for finding Jack's death certificate.

David Higham Associates for permission to quote from
Pip Granger's *Up West*.

The estate of Mark Benney (via Timothy Whidborne) for permission
to quote from *What Rough Beast*?

The Estate of Hubert Nicholson (c/o Eileen Nicoll) for permission to
quote from *Half My Days and Nights*.

The Editor has been unable to ascertain whether there are any
surviving relatives of Jack Neave. If anyone has any information
regarding same, please contact him through the publishers.

CONTENTS

INTRODUCTION

BY PHIL BAKER

Limping his way through the Thirties and beyond, the once-famous Ironfoot Jack was a celebrated mid-century Soho character, and the self-styled "King of Bohemia". Jack Neave's career included running nightclubs and starting a religion, but the origins of this intriguing individual are hard to pin down and not much illuminated by his own accounts of them. We know he was born in Australia around 1881 and came to Britain with his mother, who died shortly afterwards: he then spent time with his grandparents and in a boys' home or reformatory before taking to life on the road with gipsies and a fairground, working as a strongman. At some point an accident left him with one leg several inches shorter than the other, requiring a metal frame under his boot, and it is in his accounts of this that we get the true flavour of Jack. He had, he said, been bitten by a bloodhound; been in an avalanche in Tibet; had an accident tiger-hunting; been run over by a car while saving the life of a child; or had his leg bitten off by a shark while diving for pearls. The latter, as people weren't slow to notice at the time, is particularly unconvincing because the foot was still happily attached.

The fullest picture of Jack to date comes from Mark Benney, an interesting character in his own right. Benney had been a burglar but later became a sociologist, after writing his 1936 autobiography *Low Company*. Benney's 1939 book about Jack, *What Rough Beast?* — taking its title from W. B. Yeats's Antichrist poem, 'The Second Coming'—began as a biography but ended up as a more speculative "biographical fantasia", resorting to imaginative reconstruction after its more solidly witnessed first chapter. Benney remembers the first time he met Jack, "in a little underground haunt at the back of Oxford Street, within whose jungle-daubed walls there nightly gather the sort of people you will call squalid or picturesque as your inclinations run." It was a dive so low it soon called up a trippy little fantasia of its own, with a cellar-full of faces that seemed "by some horrible biological travesty, to sprout from the writhing arborescence of the frescoes behind them, to become pale misshapen fungi attached to the painted tropic vegetation of the walls." Tellingly, Jack wanted this basement written out of Benney's book: "I don't want readers to get wrong ideas about me. It's only a nacciden [sic] we met in a dive. It ain't my natchrel environment. I'm an intellectual, so say we met in the Café Royal."

Benney describes the powerful bulk of Jack's upper body, set on little underdeveloped legs, and his grandiosely dated garb—often a sign of the charlatan — "in the style of the nineteenth century savant." Jack was sporting a rather Dickensian outfit with a black morning coat or frock coat, with frayed silken lapels, together with a black velvet waistcoat, a high wing collar, and a black cravat. After failing to sell a girl a bracelet, he produced a small bottle of perfume—the recesses of his clothing were apparently full of them — and in a moment he was in full flow: "Blended it meself, I did. It's a secret, I got it from a Yogi at the Buddhist temple." As for temples, just a drop on the right temple, he said, pointing at her head, would dispel "oppression, sordidness and monotony", while a drop on the left temple — his finger moved round —"hinduces sexual desire". More miraculous still, a drop on the base of the spine had contraceptive powers.

Benney makes ignorance—ignorance, as he puts it, *an und für sich*, a term associated with Hegelian philosophy—the central theme in his study of Jack, and the effect is more than a little patronising. Nevertheless, Jack was not a man we have to feel sorry for. The writer John Lanchester remembers a story his father liked to tell about a tutor of his at university, "a Viennese professor of something or other." During a conversation about what people would have, if they could have anything at all in the world, the old professor sucked on his pipe, thought for a moment, and then said: "Well, if I could really have anything I wanted, anything at all, I think I would choose... *permanent* delusions of grandeur."

With his widespread knowledge of almost anything—antiques, philosophy, the occult — it is not surprising Jack himself was a professor; a title that was once more interesting than it is now. "How one relishes the professors of yesterday!" writes E. S. Turner in his *ABC of Nostalgia*. He cites a professor with a boxing kangaroo, a professor of competition solutions, and professors of self-defence, phrenology, ventriloquism, ballroom dancing and flea circuses. Peddlers of quack medicines were often "professors", and then there were more distinguished individuals such as Professor Finney, whose speciality was setting himself on fire and diving off seaside piers. Jack was Professor Neave L.P.A. or, as the brass nameplate outside his digs had it, according to Benney, Professor Curio L.P.A. (L.P.A. stood for "Lecturer in Physiolomy [sic] and Astrology").

The strength of Jack's personality was such that a kind of force field seemed to warp the reality around him. Even the British Museum seemed to wobble slightly, faced with Jack, as Benney noticed when they visited it together. Jack liked to "keep in touch with anticks" [antiques] at the museum, particularly before he visited the street antique markets, and his route invariably led him through the now departed British Library, into the tribal art section, and finally to the Buddhas in the Indian art department ("The explanation of the 'ole phenomena of life!" he told Benney in front of a Buddha: "Superrationism! Puts the mockers on the law of chance! Karma!"). According to Jack it was only through him that the museum—with its staff being just a bunch of "stereotypes", a Jack word roughly equivalent to the "squares" of a later generation— had acquired many of its antiques, because he'd bought them himself in the Caledonian Road market. He was particularly fond of the Tibetan exhibits, pointing out a lotus as the "goetic circle" of black magic, and showing Benney a Tibetan board used for casting horoscopes, which he was able to decipher because he knew the old "Venetian script". Why it should be Venetian (Phoenician? Venusian?) is a mystery, but as Benney nicely puts it, "his ignorance never failed him on any subject."

Journalist Hubert Nicholson - who relished unusual characters, including the artist and occultist Austin Osman Spare, Jack's contemporary—was among those who felt Benney was unfair to Jack, "a kindly and fascinating character" as Nicholson remembered him. Writer Maurice Richardson, who knew Aleister Crowley, noted Jack's resemblance to Crowley in physiognomy and perhaps even character (sharing a "striking combination of pyknic physique, paranoid tendencies and hypomanic temperament—there but for the grace of the gods…). Other witnesses include jazz musician Jack Glicco, in his Soho memoir *Madness After Midnight*, who remembers Jack as known to everyone across the West End in a career that included fortune telling, antique dealing, phrenology, and being a Hyde Park orator at Speaker's Corner, as well as running nightclubs, leading to what Glicco describes as "the biggest [police] raid in the history of Soho."

George Melly and Daniel Farson—Jack figures in Farson's *Soho in the Fifties*—both found that Jack in person could be a bore. Melly elaborates: "I came to know many a famous old Bohemian bore such as Iron Foot Jack, with his pocketful of yellowing press cuttings…dressed in a wide hat, cloak and knotted scarf and smelling like a goat in rut… He had a juicy cockney accent, boasted of occult powers, and lived with a series of old crones whom he used as an excuse for hinting at Crowleyan sexual virility. 'There are occult practices,' he told me every time we met, 'that it is best the general public know nuffink abaht.'"

On a more positive and unexpected note, Ian Dury found Jack inspiring. Coming to terms with being a "raspberry" ("raspberry ripple": cripple) in a tough cockney world after childhood polio left him with a withered leg and arm, he went to Soho in the late Fifties hoping to meet the legendary Ironfoot Jack, and he wasn't disappointed: "He was a real Bohemian: long white hair, cape, iron foot. I fell in love with the whole idea of being a Bohemian, before they said 'beatnik'."

Jack's Bohemia was downmarket of the more celebrated artistic and cultural Bohemia on the nineteenth century French model, although he aspired to it; he didn't know many credible poets, composers or painters (though he knew some artists' models, and was later a model himself at art school classes). His Bohemia, be it in London, Oxford or Birmingham, was more about "the problem of existence". This was a key phrase of Jack's, and it wasn't metaphysical but economic: it involved surviving without working, scraping a living, blagging, fiddling, and generally ducking and diving in a world where people might be purveying fake horoscopes or working the three-card trick. He recalls a man rubber-stamping books "Banned from the Public Library" and selling them to tourists who hoped they were pornographic, and Jack Glicco remembers Ironfoot Jack himself selling "The World's Most Daring Book on Sex and Marriage" by mail order, posting out copies of the Bible.

It was what William Burroughs would call a carny world, a freakish place with its fly-by-night showmanship and its own language and categories of people. Jack remembers the argot of "polary", relative of the fairground workers "parlyaree" and the bygone queer language of "polari", and his Bohemian travelling people the "Needies", rootless and chronically skint but enjoying life, as opposed to "flatties", who were roughly what a later generation would call "squares".

Jack's most successful enterprises were the founding of cults or mystery schools, notably the Children of the Sun in 1915, which had a basement flatits "Studio Temple"—on Charlotte Street. When this closed, Jack turned it into the School of Magic (Professor Curio's School of Magic, no less). He was a self-appointed expert on the esoteric, and he kept up his involvement with the field between the wars with his 1931 School of Wisdom, at first based in Goodge Street and then moving to a basement in New Oxford Street at number 89, beneath a bankrupt tailor's shop. Jack was a fount of occult lore, with what Mark Benney remembers as his "amazing cosmology" ("more fantastic than any written fantasia of the unconscious") mixing "the Law of Mutations, the Zodiac, Nirvana and the Black Mass." He solemnly told Benney that the bed-bugs in Wormwood Scrubs prison were inhabited by the souls of dead warders.

Benney remembers that everything in Jack's world – perfumes, trinkets, jewels, colours – seemed to have almost talismanic significance, along with "Books, art-objects—these are the receptacles of Beauty, which, together with the Buddha and Black magic, make up the strange trinity of Jack's gods." Beauty, Buddhism, and magic: it is a heady combination, with its drive towards exoticism and transcendence, overlapping at the time with the cultural fall-out of Aestheticism and Theosophy. The young Austin Spare drank at similar fountains. The occult has a perennial appeal, and Jack's book shows it vibrating across London in a would-be esoteric underground; often literally underground because, as Jack makes clear, it all seemed to happen in cellars and basements.

The revelation of this underground, a strange spiritual hinterland existing mainly in the seedier parts of the West End but spreading as far afield as the Mauve Circle in Richmond, the School of Karma in Kensington, and the Tibetan School of Wisdom in Notting Hill, is one of the fascinations of Jack's book. We meet characters such as the White Yogi of Old Compton Street, with his goddess statue and his upside-down décor, and Snuffie with his "Temple" in Drummond Street, complete with pentagram and crystal. When the Dome on Rathbone Place—which seems to have been the underground dive where Benney first met Jack, the one with the writhing walls—closed down, it turned into the Last Chance, an Indian tea shop with a tapestry of Ganesh on the wall, and became a meeting place for people interested in the philosophy of yoga. Little Buddhas and joss sticks are all over the place in Jack's London, and the Bohemian decor of these esoteric and occult haunts also includes rugs or curtains on the walls, Chinese dragons on curtains and dressing gowns, and anything oriental or ethnic. Jack's most celebrated and notorious venture—leading to a prison sentence—was the Caravan Club, in a basement at 81 Endell Street, and here the atmospheric props included five tribal masks from his own flat and an elaborately carved Burmese chair. There was also an incense burner hanging from the ceiling, but all of it was gone and vanished for ever by the time Jack got out of prison: "I've often thought to go down to Scotland Yard and have them give me a photograph of the interior of it, because unless you saw a photograph of how this place was decorated you could hardly believe it."

Jack owed much of his later celebrity to the Caravan Club affair, but he is quite discreet in this book about what the real issue was. Jack Glicco, in his generally sensational and salacious book, precedes his account of the Club—which announced itself as catering "for lovers of Art and Beauty"—with rumours of female models stripping naked under the influence of hypnosis at the School of Wisdom, implicitly floating a suggestion that the Club was showing more Art and Beauty than the law allowed.

Writing in his book *Queer London: Perils and Pleasures in the Sexual Metropolis 1918–1957*, Matt Houlbrook is less vague. In his account, Jack "deliberately cultivated a queer clientele", with a club that was "unambiguously intended to draw queer men's patronage. Inside they could dance, kiss, and have sex. In six weeks it acquired 445 members and was visited by 2004 people." During the 1934 trial, "Rex vs. Jack Neave and others, charged with keeping a disorderly house", Jack defended his right to run a queer venue on "scientific" grounds, invoking phrenology, but Rex was having none of it and Jack was sentenced to twenty months hard labour.

Jack seems to have emerged with his spirit intact, but the world he knew was changing, and much of it was swept away after the Second World War. The Caledonian Road market (source of "clutter" for dealing, or as we would say "junk") disappeared; the Welfare State mercifully came in and saved Jack from becoming a destitute tramp in his old age; and economic efficiency caught up with the basements and cellars of Bohemia, which were widely taken over by manufacturing and storage and ceased to be a cheap habitat for alternative living.

Jack's Bohemia was "gone with the wind", as he puts it, and this book is its obituary, with its detailed topography of dives and cafes. As a work of London lowlife it goes alongside books such as Benney's *Low Company*, John Worby's 1939 *Spiv's Progress* (with chapters like "A Flat in Shaftesbury Avenue" and "Snide—Toots and Mr X—Devil Worshippers"), and even Heathcote Williams's *The Speakers*, a study of Hyde Park orators from a couple of decades later.

And as for the phenomenon that was Jack himself, he is probably more interesting to read about than he was to be near for too long: he seems to have made up for anything he lacked in personal hygiene by his unsinkable self-regard. But he also seems to have been essentially a kind man, and in his way a positive spirit in the world. Even Mark Benney's affably damning picture of him occasionally throws up strange, irreducible details such as his eyes: his "great grey candid eyes, mild and seraphic as a child."

Benney's emphasis on Jack's ignorance is not dispelled by the present book, with Ennemoser Levy for Eliphas Levi, and crystal gazing invented—we are told—by Dr. Kelly of Cambridge, which seems to be a confusion of Dr. Dee and his skrying sidekick Kelley. To be fair, the effect must be exacerbated by the fact that this manuscript had its origin in dictation: Jack was taped while the artist Timothy Whidborne painted his picture, and Whidborne's secretary transcribed the tapes, so even if Jack had known Nina Hamnett's correct name, which is dubious, she was always likely to come out as Nina Hamlet. Calipe and Dentons of Poland Street is evidently Calipe, Dettmer and Co, jewellers, who were at number 21, but a few mysteries remain. We're told, for example, that there was a market selling old paintings at Burlington Road, Holborn, which is a non-existent location, so where was it?

Instead of his ignorance, I'd like to remember Jack for the extraordinary amount that he knew. He knew about his London; and about the many queer (in the older sense of the word) characters who inhabited it; and about the many and varied ways of doing battle with "the problem of existence"; and about ways of life which even offer premonitions, here and there, of the slightly later "counter-culture." And here it is, as he might have said himself, all wrote down for you.

the Silence, it
for it cannot
speak! apply
By the human
mind, Practical
application to
every thing.
Organization
of 'cause' Prepresents
By whom,
creation in the
given field, and
the creators

Ironfoot's note book for *The Surrender of Silence*, 1936.

EDITOR'S INTRODUCTION

BY COLIN STANLEY

I understand from the artist Timothy Whidborne[1] that, during the many sessions he spent with Jack when painting his portrait in the mid-1950s, he dictated *The Surrender of Silence* onto a tape recorder. Arrangements were then made, by Whidborne's secretary, for the manuscript to be typed. The original was retained by Whidborne who undertook to try and find a publisher. Jack was given the carbon copy which he carried around with him in his bag before entrusting it, in 1957, to the author Colin Wilson whose book *The Outsider* (London: Victor Gollancz) had been one of the sensations of 1956.

Because the memoir was transcribed directly from a recording, I have been forced to make some alterations and corrections when editing but have tried, as much as possible, to retain the essence of Jack's story. He provides few precise dates (except to state that the manuscript was dictated in 1956) and jumps backwards and forwards from one period to another. For this reason I have tried, wherever possible, to work out approximate dates and have included them in the footnotes.

The Surrender of Silence provides little information about Jack's early life and the circumstances surrounding his imprisonment in the mid-1930s. As Jack points out, this is covered in Mark Benney's biography: *What Rough Beast?: a biographical fantasia on the life of Professor J. R. Neave, otherwise known as Ironfoot Jack* (London: Peter Davies, 1939).

---

1   Timothy Whidborne, born 1927. British artist famous for his portrait of Queen Elizabeth II in 1969. He was a pupil of Pietro Annigoni.

Because this book is now difficult to obtain, a short biographical sketch may be useful before plunging into Jack's memoirs.

Jack Rudolph Neave was born in Sydney, Australia on November 4, 1881. His mother dreamed of returning to England and in 1891 she got her wish when, with Jack and his father, she set sail for London. His father jumped ship when they docked at Marseilles and Jack and his mother were forced to complete the journey without him. They lived with Jack's grandparents in London until his mother died just one year later in 1892. Unfairly blaming the boy for his mother's death, his grandparents placed him in Walworth Boys' Home on March 16, 1893, when he was 11 years old.

Unhappy, he absconded and hit the road. There he was befriended by gipsies and other travellers, making himself useful by helping out at fairgrounds and markets. He told fortunes using a system of numerology, sold charms and performed as an escapologist to make ends meet, touring seaside resorts all around the country until 1909 when, in frustration, after several run-ins with the local authorities, he threw his chains and straitjacket into the sea at Blackpool.

It was in that fateful year of 1909 that Jack suffered the accident that left him disabled with one leg shorter than the other. An account of how this happened depended on Jack's mood, and to whom he was speaking: he may have been shot in the leg whilst smuggling, or bitten by a shark, a lion, or a rampant bloodhound. Or trapped under a boulder or under a motor vehicle when rescuing a child playing in the street. Whatever the truth may have been, a windfall came his way as a result, enabling him to purchase a caravan and pony and travel the highways and byways plying his trade as "Professor Curio, Lecturer in Astrology, Evolution and the Occult Sciences." This windfall also furnished him with a surgical boot with the iron extension below the sole, long black theatrical cloak and wide-brimmed hat that became a trademark for the rest of his days.

With a woman called Zenobia in tow, he travelled around the fairgrounds exhibiting home-made "Marvels of the Universe" in a side-show. Zenobia became "The Incredible Leopard Woman" covered in paw-shaped spots stencilled onto her body using an appropriately carved cork dipped in iodine. Hubert Nicholson (1908–1966), as a young boy, recalls witnessing this "phenomenon":

One year (I was perhaps about nine) there was a side-show I longed to see. I do not know why, or what I expected. It was called "The Leopard Lady", and I begged my mother to let me go. She gave me the twopence and stood outside while I went in. It was late afternoon, October twilight, and the tent was empty, except for a pale woman in a purple robe who was vomiting horribly on to the ground. I stood and stared. Out of the shadows came a man with waist-length black hair, a black cloak flapping like wings, a cravat, ringed fingers, piercing eyes and a short leg with an iron extension clamped to his boot.

"What do you want?" he said.

I was really frightened, but I had paid my twopence and as a good Yorkshire boy I was not going out till I had seen what I went to see.

"The Leopard Lady," I answered.

He spoke to the woman, in a *parlari*, a showfolk's jargon, that I did not understand. She pulled herself together, wiped her mouth, un-fastened her robe.

I saw a lot of flesh, all marked with yellow-brown spots in roughly the form of an animal's paw-marks. The showman said something about the woman's mother having been frightened by a leopard. I concluded he meant something unmentionable; and also that it was not true. As a show it disappointed me greatly; as a glimpse of a life I could only darkly conjecture, it haunted me like a nightmare for years.

As soon as I had looked and been invited to touch her spotted limbs, the Leopard Lady folded her purple robe round her again and went back to the business of being sick. I hurried out of the tent and was promptly sick also.

That was my first meeting with Ironfoot Jack ("Professor" Jack Neave), "last of the long-haired showmen", "king of the underworld", etc., whom I was to know later in Soho as a kindly and fascinating character, a man deserving of better report than his over-dazzling biographer Mark Benney has given him in *What Rough Beast?* (*Half My Days and Nights: autobiography of a reporter*. London: William Heinemann Ltd., 1941, page 18–19.)

When Zenobia decided that enough was enough and absconded, Jack abandoned the fairgrounds and headed for London to live in a garret on the Gray's Inn Road. He became a Hyde Park orator and toyed with the idea of joining an anarchist-communist group. At one of the meetings he was staggered to discover that his long-lost father was the speaker. When his father disowned him for a second time it was a shattering blow. It ended his association with the anarchists and heralded a dark period in Jack's life when he became virtually a down-and-out.

In 1915, however, he fell-in with a well-off widow by the name of Mrs Balbus and was persuaded by her to found a new religion called "The Children of the Sun". Initial meetings were held at her house but as the congregation grew a basement flat was acquired in Charlotte Street in the West End. When this was disbanded he retained the flat which became the home of "Professor Curio's School of Magic". Entrance was free with nightly lectures and refreshments: "Open to 2 a.m." The manageress was Mrs J. Neave, Jinny, who he had met when they were sheltering from an air raid during the First World War, and married around 1924. Mark Benney described the many and various ways he employed to "solve the problem of existence" at this time:

For the next few years Jack's economic life was much too obscure and complicated to be related with any coherence. The immediate object of his life had become one of rent-finding; he was passionately attached to his "studio," and made frenzied efforts to retain it. To this end he became many things at once. He bought and sold all manner of objects, he read horoscopes, he tipped horses, he interpreted dreams, he hawked cough-cures, he made cheap jewellery, he blended scents. He was to be found conducting credulous strangers on tours through London's "night-life"; or lecturing, with the aid of a bored chimpanzee, on Evolution and Mormonism. For a short while he drove a flourishing trade in vanishing ink, which he sold to aspiring crooks with the advice that they use it to sign hire-purchase agreements. Again, he had a temporary phase of prosperity when he hit upon the idea of advertising in low journals the sale of "The World's Most Daring Book on Problems of Sex and Marriage–By More than a Hundred Eminent Authorities": a description of the Holy Bible which enabled him to sell by mail-order, at five hundred per cent profit, a job-lot he had picked up from a bankrupt missionary society. (*What Rough Beast?* p. 286)

Pip Granger (1947–2012) provides further examples of Jack's many 'cons':

He advertised for people to send ten bob…to receive the secret of making money 'by return of post'. When he got an enquiry, he'd reply promptly with the advice: "Do what I did!" Another scam was to advertise his patent fly killer. Again, on receipt of five shillings …he'd post back two small blocks of wood, one marked 'A' and the other 'B' and instructions to "Place the fly on block A and whack it hard with block B." (*Up West.* Long Preston: Magna Large Print Books, 2009, p. 201–2.)

By these and other means he was able to set-up his "School of Wisdom" in 1931. Musician Jack Glicco (real name: Jacob Gluckstein) commented:

> The brochure that advertised it promised that lectures would be given on Yoga, Superstition, Graphology, Art, Evolution, Zoroastra and Hypnotism. Jack, who had now added the title "Professor" in front of his name, was the chief tutor, while his instructors placed letters after their names: "FKAL," "PHE" and "LPA"–though what they were supposed to mean has long since been forgotten.
>
> The pupils began to flock to the 'school' when the word went around that the lecturer on hypnotism could make a woman strip herself naked while under the influence, and that the Art tutor was particularly graphic when instructing his scholars on painting the female body beautiful–and nude. (*Madness After Midnight.* London: Elek Books, 1952, p. 104–5.)

This was followed by "La Boheme Literary Society" in a garret high above Charing Cross Road, the "Albatross Studio", the "Café Lounge" and, in the summer of 1934, the ill-fated "Caravan Club' established for lovers of "Art and Beauty". When this was raided by the police in August of that year, he was charged at Bow Street Magistrates' Court with:

> Having on July 25, 26 and 27, unlawfully kept and maintained a place on Endell Street for the purpose of exhibiting to any person willing to pay for admission to the said place, divers lewd, scandalous, bawdy and obscene performances and practices to the manifest corruption of his Majesty's liege subjects.

Jack Glicco continued the story:

> More than 150 people were charged, including Ironfoot Jack. At the second hearing at Bow Street the police brought no evidence against seventy-six of the defendants, who had been accused of aiding and abetting, and they were immediately discharged. Of the remainder, twenty-six were formally committed for trial at the Old Bailey. (*Madness After Midnight*, p. 105–6.)

He appeared on September 4, 1934. The trial attracted a great deal of media interest, the Sunday tabloids in particular. According to *The Times*, a police officer, who had attended the club in plain clothes, testified that: "Some men were made up like women and acted like women. One started to dance as a woman would be expected to dance. Men were cuddling and embracing..." (*The Times*, Sept 6, 1934, p. 9). Despite Jack's denial that any such dancing took place he was found guilty and sentenced, on October 26, to twenty months hard labour in Wormwood Scrubs.

When Mark Benney, researching his book, met him at the Dome café, Rathbone Place in 1938, he described him as follows:

> A massively-built man, with a tremendous width of shoulders, his bulk was robbed of all impressiveness by the short, puny legs, the right withered and furnished with a clumsy iron boot. His features had a large flabbiness, and would have been obscene but for the great grey candid eyes, mild and seraphic as a child's. Every visible pore of his skin was clogged with the accumulated grease of years. His dress was in the style of the nineteenth-century savant. A three-quarter-length morning coat of black cloth with frayed silken lapels surmounted a black velvet waistcoat. Black trousers concertina'd down to his boots; and his double chin, as he bent over his work, half-obscured the winged

collar and black cravat which was spread out, beneath its cameo fastener, to hide the grubbiness of the shirt beneath it. (*What Rough Beast?* p. 3)

The Surrender of Silence concentrates mainly on the period following his release from prison: the Second World War and afterwards until 1956. His letters to Colin Wilson, included as Appendix 3, give some details of Jack's movements between then and his death on September 29, 1959 at St Columba's Hospital in Hampstead. Two late interviews were printed in *Reynold's News* (see Appendix 4) and *The Spectator*, the latter published on March 27, 1959.[2]

Colin Wilson and Ironfoot Jack:

In 2009 the University of Nottingham acquired my vast collection of the printed works of the English existentialist philosopher and author Colin Wilson (1931–2013). As his bibliographer I had built-up the collection over more than three decades and it had become too big for my house to accommodate. A few years before his death I suggested to him, and his wife Joy, that they consider depositing his papers and manuscripts at the same location with the aim of creating a centre for the study of his work and, in the summer of 2012, the first tranche of around eighty manuscripts, and several files of correspondence, was transferred from their home in Cornwall to the safety of the Manuscripts and Special Collections store at the University.

In the ensuing years I have continued the task of sorting, and making ready for transfer, nearly sixty years of Colin Wilson's work: papers, journals, correspondence and manuscripts, including the

2 Full text can be accessed at: http://archive.spectator.co.uk/article/27th-march-1959/11/roundabout

handwritten manuscript of *The Outsider,* one of the most iconic books of the twentieth century.

I was intrigued to find, among his papers, the carbon copy of Ironfoot Jack's manuscript *The Surrender of Silence* along with a folder containing photographs, press cuttings and letters.[3] Some of these letters are reproduced in Appendix 3 and they reveal that Jack, having completed his manuscript in 1956, left it with Colin, sometime in 1957, in the hope that he could find a publisher for it. Naturally Colin turned first to his own publisher Victor Gollancz who, judging by a rather curt note scribbled on a compliments slip, was not at all impressed. In 1960, shortly after Jack's death, the manuscript was in the hands of Skelton Robinson Limited, a London publisher who was keen enough to send it out to an editor. The many handwritten corrections and suggestions that appear on the manuscript date from this time. Unfortunately, Skelton Robinson ceased trading in 1961 and so Colin's efforts were thwarted. With Jack deceased, and therefore no longer able to benefit financially from the project (he had hoped that royalties from its publication would supply him with a comfortable old-age), the incentive to find a publisher was gone. I presume Colin, understandably, set it aside to concentrate on his own work.

Colin Wilson first came to London in June 1951 and was sometimes to be found around Soho. Here he met and befriended several other budding writers: Bill Hopkins (1928–2011), Stuart Holroyd (1933–), Alexander Trocchi (1925–1984), Laura Del Rivo (1934–) and the poet John Rety (1930–2010) who edited the coffee-bar literary magazine *The Intimate Review,* famously Colin's first publisher. He must have met Ironfoot Jack at this time because Jack was very much a celebrity figure, often to be found in the French coffee house on Old Compton Street. Also in Soho, Colin met an out-of-work actor by the name of Charles Belchier (aka Russell), a Bohemian, whose memoir *The Other Side of*

3   These are now available for consultation at the University of Nottingham.

Town,[4] was adapted by Colin into Part One of his 1961 novel *Adrift in Soho*. Jack features in both Belchier's memoir and Colin's novel. Indeed he is the only character in the novel to retain his real name. In *The Other Side of Town*, Jack is to be found in the Wheatsheaf pub, Rathbone Place (still in existence) and later the Café Alex in Soho: "His black cloak and inevitable high-collared cravat gave him the air of a Mephistophelian Santa Claus."

Colin Wilson had originally intended to dedicate *Adrift in Soho* to Jack but was dissuaded from doing so, possibly by Gollancz, and the novel was dedicated instead to "James" i.e. Charles Belchier, who features in the novel as James Compton Street. The hero is Harry Preston, a young man very much like Colin himself, who had newly arrived in London from the provinces:

> An hour later, I sat in a café in Old Compton Street and drank tea…I was watching an old man who sat at a table in the corner, snipping bits of brass wire and making them into earrings by hanging beads on them and twisting them expertly with a pair of pliers. He had a broad, good natured face and long grey hair that hung down to his shoulders, and he wore what seemed to be a very old and tattered cloak over his shoulders. From his concentration on his task, I presumed he was one of those taciturn men whose eccentricity is a sign of complete indifference to society…(It was only later that I learned I could not have been more mistaken in my idea of his character.) (*Adrift in Soho*. London: Pan Books, 1964, p. 40)

A few pages later, Jack is introduced to him when he gate-crashes the hilarious scene in Osky's kitchen-less fish and chip 'restaurant'. The idea

4   This was another manuscript I found among Colin Wilson's papers, the full text of which I published in a booklet entitled *The Writing of Colin Wilson's 'Adrift in Soho'* (Nottingham: Paupers' Press, 2016). The original is kept at the University of Nottingham.

for this scene was almost certainly gleaned from Jack himself who says in *The Surrender of Silence* that he had heard that such an establishment *had* actually existed at one time. Pip Granger asserted that Jack actually ran it *himself*:

> He rented a semi-derelict building where the electricity had been cut off. Undaunted, Jack arranged to have paraffin lamps liberated from local night-watchmen, and lit the place with those. Impressive menus were provided, in French no less, to add a little class, but every item on them, bar one, was crossed out due to 'shortages' and 'rationing'. The one dish left was '*poisson et pommes frites*'. When the diners duly ordered, Jack would yell the order into the non-existent kitchen and 'a lad' would sprint down to the nearest chippie, grab the requisite portions of fish and chips, sprint back, dump them on plates and then Jack, with the great dignity of a seasoned *maître d'hôtel*, would serve them…Needless to say the restaurant closed after a few short weeks. (*Up West*, p. 202–3)

Daniel Farson (1927–1997) included that story in his *Soho in the Fifties* (London: Michael Joseph Ltd, 1987) but doubted its veracity. Dan, however, was one of the "new generation" of post-war Sohoites who considered Jack to be "…a dreadful old bore…". George Melly (1926–2007), in the second part of his autobiography, *Rum, Bum and Concertina* (London: Weidenfeld & Nicolson, 1977), concurred adding: "He had a juicy Cockney accent, boasted of occult powers and lived with a series of old crones whom he used as an excuse for hinting at a Crowleyian sexual virility."

Despite these inevitable put-downs by a 'younger' generation, *The Surrender of Silence* stands as a remarkable document of a way of life that has gone forever: "It will be a sensation to modern society how the other half lived in those dreamy days gone by…" he wrote in a letter to

Colin Wilson. Indeed, it is difficult to think how anyone could make such a living today.

After World War Two, and the introduction of the Welfare State, Jack could see the writing on the wall: "The last World War shattered everything: Bohemian cafés, five shilling a week basements and cellars, camping out on London Commons. Those days are over now…and I do not think that situation will develop again…"[5] By the 1950s most of the characters that he wrote about had gone: many were killed in the air raids, others drifted away from a Soho that was changing rapidly. Jack, however, stayed true to his calling…right up to the end:

> I have written *The Surrender of Silence* not so much for my material gain but to the memory of a glorious past of Bohemian life which is now gone… leaving behind only memories and a brief spell of passion and strife. To a Bohemian this is what they call life…

You may not consider it to be the "sensation" that Jack predicted but, at the very least, it's an extraordinary and highly entertaining adventure story.

Colin Stanley,
Nottingham, January 2017.

5   Despite what Jack wrote it should be noted that, legend has it, Colin Wilson himself slept in a waterproof sleeping bag on Hampstead Heath whilst writing *The Outsider* in 1955.

THE SURRENDER
OF SILENCE

THE MEMOIRS OF IRONFOOT JACK

KING OF THE BOHEMIANS

Annotations by Colin Stanley

EARLY LIFE ON THE ROAD

I have decided to call this book *The Surrender of Silence* because it is the outcome of years of struggle to survive; of solving the problem of existence by various and curious methods not known today to the general public. Most of the people I am talking about led a precarious life and obtained their livelihood from day to day by many different methods. They had their own peculiar philosophy and attitude towards life. They had no desire to achieve even semi-security. They worked to live; they did not live to work.

I became a member of this fraternity. I became acquainted with gipsies, with show people, with buskers (that is, the people who travel about the country playing musical instruments), with people who entertained the public by performing in the city, on fair grounds and market places...and with a variety of "fiddles"—that is, some dubious methods of obtaining the means of life. I intend to describe them in this book.

Then there were other characters who were known as "Needies". Now these Needies, also entertainers, were not pure gipsies, but they led a wandering life and they obtained their livelihood by travelling from town to town. They had a language of their own which was known by the wandering buskers as the

"Jogars Polary."[1] This language was handed down verbally from generation to generation amongst these people; some market workers could understand it and some gipsies could understand it, but it was entirely different from the gipsy language.

Now this period of my life I was living with gipsies who lived in tents and were solving the problem of existence, travelling from one fair to another, by telling fortunes. This knowledge I obtained from the gipsies.

I was very alert at this period of my life, and I was also very curious to find out why the community was split up into various sections such as the possessing class, the middle class, the working class, the tramps and the vagrants, the wanderers and the Bohemians.

Now this word "Bohemian" is a very serious word, because its main meaning is that it covers particular characters whose attitude towards life is that they only work to live and they don't live to work—and they have no desire for any material achievements apart from living from day to day as they can, in complete harmony, indulging in the enjoyments which they create for themselves and not in the enjoyments created for them by society.

At this period of my life all the spare money I got, which was over and above my needs I spent buying second-hand books to read. I'd heard theories that, whatever circumstances one found oneself in, this was your Destiny: and this I could not believe, and was determined to try and find out what was actually the cause. In the course of years, I waded through volumes of literature. I listened to all the political speakers whom I could manage to listen to, and also all the religious speakers I could possibly listen to; also the free-thinkers, and people with various

1   I think Jack means "Jogger's parlari": the language of entertainers.

fantastic religious theories. I brought into my studies Literature, Music, Art, and Philosophy. I studied as hard as I could study.

At this period of my life—I was about twenty-five[2]—I met a performing hand-cuff King, who had been travelling about the country for fifteen years performing and escaping from a strait-jacket and hand-cuffs, performing to the public on market places and fair grounds. His name was Tim; he was getting on— he was about fifty-four—and he himself had also waded into a good deal of dynamic literature.

However, he gave me the secrets of how to escape from hand-cuffs and how to escape from a strait-jacket. I made myself a strait-jacket out of canvas and leather and got myself some ratchet hand-cuffs, and found that by this method of solving the problem of existence I could earn a very comfortable livelihood from day to day. Whereas I was making just about enough money to survive out of fortune- telling, I found that by being an Escapologist I could earn in those days—quite comfortably— five pounds a week. That was performing three times a day and going around the crowds and collecting. In the summertime I made for seaside resorts; I visited Blackpool for three seasons, and performed on the sands.

Now this coincidence I consider was the finest thing could have happened to me, because with the surplus money I bought myself a very nice tent, all the comfortable sleeping accommodation for the tent, and a pony and trap. For once in my life I was organized.

My attitude towards life then—well, I was contented, but I was inwardly conscious that I must prepare myself for the changing of events. I was always conscious that events were

2   Probably around 1906.

continually changing, so in order to counteract this I had to have more knowledge. I started wading deeper into Literature. I read *The Origin of the Species*, by Darwin, *The Wealth of Nations* by Adam Smith, and *The Decline and Fall of the Roman Empire*, by Gibbon. I read a few philosophers: Voltaire, Schopenhauer and Nietzsche, and I read Ingersoll's *Essays*.[3] Then I got hold of a book which disturbed me more than anything: it was entitled *The Martyrdom of Man*, by Winwood Reade.[4] This book gave me, so far as I was concerned, a clearer insight into the Evolution of Events. And any literature which advocated that the situation that I was in—and the situation that many other characters were in—was the outcome of Destiny, I disregarded.

While all this was going on, I travelled with my pony and trap between Blackpool and Brighton, Southampton and Scarborough, and Scarborough to Newcastle-on-Tyne. I visited the big industrial cities, Sheffield and Manchester, Birmingham and Leeds, but I preferred performing in little rural towns such as Banbury.

After five years performing on fair grounds and market places with chains and hand-cuffs and a strait-jacket (in the wintertime I'd find myself a fair ground somewhere that had pulled in for the winter, and I'd perform for some showman who had a side-show and that got me through the winter), the book *The Martyrdom of Man*, by Winwood Reade, threw me into another channel of thought. I decided to study the Occult Sciences and find an Occult Science, apart from Astrology from which I could get a comfortable existence.

3   Robert Green Ingersoll (1833–1899) U.S. lawyer, political leader, orator known as 'The Great Agnostic' whose *Essays and Criticisms* was published in 1897.
4   William Winwood Reade (1838–1875): British explorer, philosopher and historian.

Ironfoot the escapologist, 1913.

During my last performance with the chains and hand-cuffs at Blackpool, I was arrested for obstruction and warned off the fore-shore. For years there had been a law that people who performed to the public—conjurors, ventriloquists, acrobats, buskers—were supposed to be allowed to perform on the fore-shore at Blackpool when the tide was out. When the tide was out a hundred and twenty-five yards from the fore-shore this was considered to be "No Man's Land". The tide used to remain out at different periods of the day for two or three hours, which allowed all these various characters who obtained their living by performing to the public to perform on No Man's Land—collect a nice crowd of people around them—and so earn a comfortable existence.

Now, as I've said before, I wandered about for five years performing with a strait-jacket and hand-cuffs. I also performed in various places in the suburbs of London, but I was more or less convinced that I could find some other method of existing. Of the five years during which I was performing and wandering about the country, the first three years in the different towns and villages, I was welcomed and allowed a good deal of freedom. I also had some good write-ups and some good publicity in various towns I went into; there was an article about me in one of the Blackpool papers during this period of my life, and also an article about me in Oxford when I performed on Carfax, in front of the Randolph Hotel.

In these days, if you were a performer—a public entertainer performing in the open—it was necessary for you to go the Town Hall in whatever town you were in and see the Mayor or the Mayoress. They were very sympathetic towards performers and you were permitted to perform for three days and then move on to another town. Some market places, where I went to

8

perform, I had to pay a few shillings to be allowed to perform, and at some fairgrounds I also had to pay a few shillings to be allowed to perform.

But during the last few years out of the five—the wandering about the country and performing years—somehow the country town authorities and also the shopkeepers became very antagonistic towards performers, and we found ourselves being moved on and chased all over the place. There was also another complicated situation: in many cases, when you performed in one town you'd have to be very steady with your finances because it might be three or four days before you found another town you could perform in.

I made a terrific speech in the dock when I was in Blackpool. I was fined and the performers and buskers warned off of "No Man's Land", so I went to the end of the pier and threw the hand-cuffs and the chains into the sea...

During this period of my life I'd been buying various books on Numerology. I'd also read the memoirs of Pythagoras, and I started to draw up a pamphlet of Numerology according to my calculations. I also found in various bookshops some very interesting pamphlets on Numerology, and got myself a nice board painted and called myself "Britain's Celebrated Numerologist."

After I'd had the four dominating numbers calculated, I drew up a pamphlet which was a slight prediction. It was a very dynamic reading worked for some considerable time, until I accumulated four very powerful formulas on Advice. I always enquired the date of a person's birth, and my Four Advices applied to the four quarters of the Seasons—the first three months, the second three months, the third three months, and the fourth three months.[5]

By this method of obtaining an existence I could only earn about three pounds a week, but of course in those days three was like nine pounds now. I was a wandering aristocrat of the road.

While all this was going on I spent most of my time with my friends, and my friends were buskers, intellectual tramps, and intellectual vagabonds. There were quite a few on the road in those days—show people, gipsies, buskers, and Needies.

Now while all this was going on I started to wade deeply into the Occult Sciences. I made a great study of Phrenology; the founders were Dr. Gyle and Dr. Spurgeon. Then I got hold of Lavarty's *Physiognomy*[6] which shows the characteristics of a person from the features: the shape of the nose, the shape of the eyes, the shape of the mouth, and the shape of the ears; and Phrenology is the science of the shape of the cranium and the various bumps on the back of the head. I thought, "Well, I'll experiment with this," and I had a board with "England's Celebrated Physiognomist" on it and I got an artist friend of mine to put side-faces, noses, lips and ears on the board.

This only lasted for a week because I discovered that the Public had more confidence in Numerology than Physiognomy, and as a matter of fact there's more fascinated by Numerology than there was by Astrology.

Then I studied Graphology, and read what literature I could get on that; and that was supposed to be the science of handwriting. Card reading, I was quite acquainted with, because I'd learned that art thoroughly from the gipsies. I also read what

5   See Appendix 1.
6   Jack almost certainly meant Johann Kasper Lavater (1741–1801) who was a Swiss poet, theologian and physiognomist. His book on physiognomy was first published between 1775 and 1778.

books I could get out on Palmistry but this antagonized me because it advocated the theory of Destiny.

Now I always had a very good idea through my own intuition and sense perception (of which I've always possessed a goodly share), and I've always held this theory: that an individual to a great extent is the architect of his own destiny, according to the decisions he makes. However, it was not until I started wading into Oriental Philosophy that this particular theory was backed up. I was still unsatisfied with the theory that the destiny of the individual in society was the outcome of Destiny, although I'd gone through a lot of theories which advocated that if things are what they are, they can't be anything else but what they are. But after studying Oriental Philosophy I discovered that events and things could be entirely different, either for better or for worse; that they were to a great extent determined by the decisions of individuals. I became fascinated by Theosophy, and read Mme Blavatsky's *Secret Doctrine*.

I used to get great amusement by going to all these other characters that I met on the road, in fair grounds and market places, who were giving readings with the crystal, with Palmistry, Clairvoyance and Psychometry. I met a Chinese woman who spoke fluent English and definitely had had a very good schooling, who obtained a livelihood by Psychometry. There is no formula laid down for Psychometry. You take an article from the crowd and you speculate on the disposition of the person it belonged to and what might have happened in the past and what was liable to happen in the future. She was getting a very comfortable living because there were no other characters competing against her in her particular method of reading. I had a chat with her, and she had a great knowledge of Psychology:

she'd read Freud and Adler and Havelock Ellis, and I'd also studied them to an extent. In some period of her life she'd been acquainted with the medical profession and she was a very keen observer of Ideology. She was living with a character who called himself "The Professor," because he gave lectures on obscure subjects. There is no doubt that he was well-travelled, and he gave private lectures on primitive civilizations. He knew quite a lot about the Conquest of Mexico, the Incas of Peru and a brief history of the Polynesian Islands. She was quite a bit younger than he, and he was getting on in years.

They had a fine caravan; it wasn't expensive but comfortable, motor driven. I only met them once, on Southampton Common one Bank Holiday, and I didn't see them anymore in my wanderings. She recommended me not to study Black and White Magic but to study the history of it, so I read *The History of Magic* by Ennemoser Levy.[7] Then I went on to study Auto-Suggestion, and then I got hold of some pamphlets which were written by a character who called himself "Cosmo," and these pamphlets consisted of formulas appertaining to Vibrations, the Law of Attitudes and the Laws of Fascination.

Now while I was wading through all this literature I had no desire to make money. I only had a desire to make a comfortable existence and enjoy my freedom, which I had. I often wondered why this terrific feeling of freedom possessed me and why I was not like other people, who were leading an orthodox and conventional life and had a desire for riches and security.

This I discovered was because I was like many of my friends who were leading a precarious life. I could not tolerate routine

7 Jack must have meant Eliphas Levi (1810–1875) the French occultist whose *The History of Magic* was first published in 1860.

of any description. I came across many characters who managed to get enough money in some morning's fiddle, and were not prepared to go on fiddling the rest of the afternoon and night to get more money to achieve some particular kind of security. Even the characters who had tents had no desire for houses or caravans, and the intellectual tramps and vagabonds had no desire for respectability. They only lived to live.

At this period of my life there was quite a lot of quack doctors on the road, and miracle-workers who would stimulate their patients by Auto-Suggestion and the Powers of Fascination. The most amazing thing about all these characters of the road was that the great percentage of them were not antagonistic towards their conditions because there was food in abundance and all these characters had the knowledge of how to manipulate a shilling or two shillings into a banquet. In those days you could buy a pound of bacon cuttings in any grocer's shop in any town or village for a penny. You could also get a half a dozen cracked eggs for a penny, already cracked for you to save you the trouble of cracking 'em. And with either a penn'orth[8] of onions or tomatoes and a loaf, and some boiled potatoes, you could make a banquet large enough for four people to enjoy.

I shall now describe how having the knowledge and the secrets of the road helped these characters because, if they woke up in a strange town completely penniless, they could always find a commodity which they could commercialize and get money to buy food. On some occasions I've done it myself when I woke up completely financially destitute.

Now if you wake up completely destitute, you go in and out of the local shops in the town, and the boarding-houses, and you

8 Bought for one penny.

ask them if they can give you a few newspapers. After scouting round for about two hours you will collect, from the citizens of the village or town, enough newspapers which you can take into any butcher's or fried-fish shop and get two or three shillings for. Now this method the characters would call "the life-saver".

The tramps and the vagabonds in these days were not wandering vagrants. They were professional vagabonds and tramps and they considered themselves the aristocrats of the open road. They made it their business to keep away from the large industrial towns and mostly were found in rural towns and villages. They were the legalized tramps and vagabonds. In the wintertime they could go from one town to another, from workhouse to workhouse. They were given a clean bed, a bath, some supper, some breakfast, and had to do a little work there cleaning the place up or chopping some wood in the wood-shed—and then they were let out on the road, if they wanted to go.

Now to be a legalized vagabond one must, by law, have a ground-sheet and blankets, or a sleeping-bag, or a ground-sheet and some overcoats. If you are caught sleeping out without a ground-sheet and without blankets, or without overcoats, you are considered a menace to the medical profession because you might get pneumonia and have to be taken to a hospital or an institute, and put doctors to a lot of unnecessary trouble. And you are also liable to get yourself in prison for being a vagrant. Another thing which was necessary was to have a silver coin of the realm in your possession.

There was also a season for these tramps and vagabonds, because they were prepared to work for the farmers in the fruit-picking and the potato-picking seasons.

To obtain good second-hand clothes was not a problem because in those days in every town and village there was rag stores and second-hand clothes shops where you could buy a clean second-hand shirt for four pence,[9] a good second-hand jacket or a pair of trousers for a shilling, and a second-hand pair of shoes for a shilling and a second-hand overcoat for a shilling. In those days, these commodities were in abundance.

Then there were lodging-houses who catered for gentlemen of the road. They were called "nethers kenners", and it was sixpence for a single bed and a shilling if you had your wife with you. And there were couples travelling about the roads in those days of all ages who, in the winter-time, made a bee-line for these travellers' lodging-houses.

And there were the vagabond hawkers who travelled about with their families and had all their belongings—their tents and their camping equipment, everything—on a perambulator. And these people with the perambulators were the Needies, who I mentioned before, and who had their own language known as Jogars Polary. It was partly Romany and also partly the language of the travelling entertainers and performers and the buskers.

Now also it has been the law that you can camp on any Rush Common in Great Britain. That is to say, if you find a piece of land by the side of the farmer's field which is not finished off and which is large enough for you to camp on—or pull a caravan on, down a lane or by the side of the road—providing you are well out of the way of the traffic on the road, you are allowed to remain there for twelve hours. And you shift your camping pitch every night.

9 Readers should note that a shilling consisted of 12 pennies and was the equivalent of 5p today.

Now after giving up my performance as an Escapologist and obtaining my livelihood with Numerology, another five years elapsed—and during this time I was studying all I could on European and Continental Occultism, including Clairvoyance and Crystal Reading. (The crystal was invented by Dr. Kelly, of Cambridge.)[10] I'd made a great study of the predictions of Nostradamus; I'd studied the history of Cagliostro; I'd read all the memoirs of the Continental and European magicians and I'd also made a great study of the alchemists and the history of Alchemy. Most of my spare time was spent—which I thoroughly enjoyed—in foraging in second-hand book shops in towns and villages.

Ten years of this kind of life had elapsed, and fortunately I came across a character who called himself "Pizzano" and considered himself a "hobo", that is, a tramp who tramps all over the world—he had been in China and in India, and he said that although he had had a year bumming around on the Continent and the Mediterranean, it didn't appeal to him in his early days. He preferred Oriental countries. He'd also been an Able Seaman on a wind-jammer. Whatever part of the world he visited in his early days—whether it was on the Continent or in the Orient—he would give addresses. He was a linguist, and could speak several Oriental languages. I found him performing on a market in Aylesbury and he was my companion for a considerable time.

He had a curious way of solving the problem of existence. He had a box of silver sand and he advised his clients to make an imprint in the sand with their hand, and he would give a reading from the impression of the hand in the sand. He also sold a

---

10 I think Jack meant Dr John Dee (1527–1608/9), the alchemist and astrologer who employed the services of Edward Kelley as his "scryer".

lucky charm which he called a "talisman," and this talisman was supposed to have been found on the ceiling of a Chinese pagoda.

And it was through him that I became very interested in Oriental Philosophy. He had done a certain amount of probing into literature, and the philosophy which he cherished more than anything was the Philosophy of Buddhism. I studied Buddhism, Zoroastrianism, Yoga, *The Vedas*, *The Mahabharata*, *The Bhagavad Gita*, and all the literature I could possibly lay my hands on pertaining to Buddhism.

Now from the study of this Philosophy I came to the conclusion that to a great extent, apart from your economic environment, it is your attitude towards life and the decisions that you make in life which make you partly—not solely, partly—the architect of your own destiny. Because if you fall in love with a woman and you go about with her and together you decide to share your lives, by the decision between yourselves, you have created some kind of destiny. If you decide to remain in one place all your life, then through your decision, as well as economic necessity, you have created a destiny for yourself. If you go to any strange town or any strange city and you adapt yourself to whatever circumstances appeal to you, then you have either consciously or unconsciously—you yourself, by *your* decision—created a destiny for yourself.

Now I did not allow this Oriental Philosophy to become an obsession whereby I wanted to convince everybody to believe in what I believed in. I came to the conclusion that whatever anybody believed in, they believed in it because it stimulated them: it gave them some kind of natural security for the conditions they were in, and it inspired them to tolerate their conditions the best that they could.

About the attitude of these aristocrats of the road: they all had terrific individuality and they all clung to the philosophy that they worked to live and they didn't live to work, as much as they could. Some were very eccentric in their attire, because it stimulated them to be outstanding individuals. And amongst all these characters of real sincerity there was a terrific hospitality. When you met them they would invite you to dine with them and to camp with them, and they handed down verbally between one another different methods of solving the problem of existence.

Now we'll get back to these Needies: as I've said before, they had their own language, and they travelled up and down the country with their perambulators and their belongings and also their families. In general, they got their living by selling wildflowers, ferns and heather; some of them used to go out collecting water cress; some were very good poachers and brought their rabbits into towns and villages and sold them round the shops, and the women—the mothers and the daughters—used to go out round the doors selling packets of lavender. Now to sell packets of lavender round the doors in little towns and villages did not require a licence. This was known as "perfume bashing". In some periods in wintertime when it was really cold and very wet and I couldn't practice my Numerology on the market place, I resorted to this as an experiment: and by selling a packet of lavender for a penny, you could earn, in those days, about two-and-six per day,[11] while so far as food was concerned, two or three could live on very substantial food for two shillings.

Then there was the tinkers: they lived in tents and led a similar life to the Needies, but their communities were bigger.

11 Two shillings and sixpence (half a crown). 12½ p today.

They went about with tents and ponies and traps; you would generally find two or three families travelling all together. They lived communally.

Now amongst them were the "china fakers". "China faking" is repairing broken plates and saucers. There were also a few scissor-grinders, who made scissor-grinding machines with one wheel and they obtained a living by travelling from town to town grinding scissors. And there were the "tiger hunters". Now the "tiger hunters" were the ones who repaired mats. They were all acquainted with "totting," which was buying up old rags and brass and cutlery and pewter, and in nearly every town and every village there was a linen store where you could sell rags. The women would always wear white or black aprons, and generally had their hair in plaits. Their favourite jewellery was a coral necklace and for a brooch they used to like a five shilling piece.

But they were not pure gipsies; they were what they call the Needies—the hawkers. Some of them travelled in caravans, but they were not expensive caravans. They were caravans that they had made themselves out of old carts, and were mostly in gipsy style, with a bow canvas top. The ones with caravans also used to travel three or four families together and would camp outside of a town in what they called the "monkery". They produced their own entertainment which mostly consisted of sitting round the camp-fire.

Now the Needies who used the perambulators and who tramped with their families from village to village and town to town mostly only camped out during the fruit-picking season. On many occasions they would camp outside of some sea-side resort and go into the resort in the daytime to get their living. Some of the young women had a basket, and in this there used to be needles and threads and thimbles and brushes, and a little bit of lace. And another method which they used was swapping one of the commodities out of the basket for some old clothes—but not rags—old clothes which were in quite good condition and which could be sold again. And these second-hand clothes were mostly sold in these travellers' lodging houses to other travellers for a few coppers.

They were always delightfully clean. They had all the washing facilities in these travellers' lodging houses, and they had a terrifically big range or plate where they could bring their food in and cook it. If any traveller arrived and he had nothing to eat there was always somebody ready to give him a meal. The hospitality and the brotherhood amongst these people was really something worthwhile.

Now we've got the Welfare State, this particular type of life is practically gone with the wind,[12] and on the road today there are very, very few towns who've got lodging houses which especially cater for these particular types of people.

They made for carnivals, regattas and for race courses, such as Epsom and Ascot...and there was a recognition between them and the gipsies; some of the Needies knew a few words of the gipsy language, and some of the gipsies knew a few words of the Jogars Polary...and some of these families brought up two or three children who followed the occupations of their parents.

But to-day these people have become practically extinct. The professional tramps have become practically extinct; the professional vagabonds have become practically extinct; the wandering people who got their living in the Occult Sciences,

12 Jack's way of saying that something has gone forever or someone has died.

such as Palmistry, Astrology and selling lucky charms, they are also becoming gradually extinct.

In those days there were certain towns where there was a warehouse where you could buy a variety of lucky charms. There were quite a few Needies who obtained their living by selling these charms—but they were all acquainted with the different methods of solving the problem of existence, that is, by obtaining enough money to buy food with.

The buskers, who wandered from town to town playing a musical instrument, were welcomed in those days in every town and village they went to. But those who are left—I meet a few of them occasionally who've been busking for thirty or forty years—today they have a very, very hard time of it. The only chance they have now is to do a bit of busking in the modern coffee houses that are developing, and it is only certain coffee houses which will allow them to play. The guitar players are more popular than the accordion players in the coffee houses, but as for playing in the street—it would be a very complicated problem for them to obtain a living today because they are chased all over the place.

In those days you could pay sixpence or a shilling a day to get your living in a market, but today most markets in Great Britain do not issue a temporary licence. The markets are more or less monopolized by the residents of the town, and they don't encourage strangers…and they certainly don't encourage any type of fortune-teller, such as Astrology, Palmistry, Crystal-Gazing or Numerology. You would have a small chance with lucky charms, providing you could talk. If you could talk, you could still obtain enough money to buy food with, with lucky charms—providing you had some other method of fitting-in, in between. You couldn't entirely rely on lucky charms. Lucky charms have always been a method which I applied when I've been in difficulties, and I've always gone to markets where they issue a temporary licence.

Now a person who could talk about a commodity on a market to a crowd is known as a "grafter", but the grafter must have some abilities as an orator. That is to say, he's either got to talk sense or he's got to put over some fantastic story. He's got to be very, very humorous and if he's selling a commodity he's got to convince the people he's talking to that they're getting something cheaper than they can get it any place else.

Unfortunately there are few markets left where they issue a temporary licence to solve the problem of existence. I don't know—there may be one or two private markets that would allow an astrologer to practise Astrology, but they are very, very far between. With lucky charms you've got more chance on a market, because a lucky charm has been manufactured and so therefore you are giving the public a commodity for their money, whereas if you are practising any of the Occult Readings you are not giving them any commodity; you are commercializing your knowledge. (One of the reasons that it is so difficult to get a livelihood by practising Astrology is because the press and all the modern papers are now giving a forecast of the influence of the Twelve Signs of the Zodiac.)

There was a very, very great charm-worker who was a friend of mine, and who was known as "The Sheik". He'd had a very good education and he'd travelled quite a lot and could speak one or two European languages—French very fluently. He was a character that would go from town to town, and from city to city; he would also take part-time jobs in cafés, such as washing dishes. He'd take a job for a month and then he'd have three months leading a precarious life; he never adapted himself to any routine work of any description. He was a very good charm worker and was in the Wembley Exhibition.[13] He called himself a Yogi and was quite acquainted with Oriental Philosophy.

I went out with him to keep him company on several occasions. Probably he's gone with the wind—I have not seen or heard of him since the last World War but I can always remember his story about his lucky charm. He had the charms in a brass cylinder and he used to put the cylinder on the ground on a piece of black velvet and do some mysterious and fantastic waving until a crowd gathered round him. And when the crowd gathered round he'd say: "Ladies and gentlemen, a lot of people are under the impression that Livingstone was the first man to penetrate Central Africa. As a matter of fact, he was not. The first man to penetrate Central Africa was a man by the name of Winwood Reade. He wrote a remarkable book which you can get in the library, which is called *The Martyrdom of Man*. He was a peculiar type of man, Winwood Reade was, because he didn't like any kind of hero worship and he didn't like notoriety. So when he came back from Africa he brought with him a skull which he presented to the Anthropologists' Society, and the skull remained in their possession for twelve years. And one day an authority on Anthropology examined the skull and discovered it was not the skull of a white man, but was the skull of an Eskimo—a physical impossibility for that particular type of skull to get into that particular part of the world. Proof that Winwood Reade was the first man to penetrate Central Africa." Then he would go on to this charm,

13 The British Empire Exhibition held at Wembley Park in 1924-5.

which was supposed to have been discovered by Winwood Reade and was known as a "talisman," and he would say that "commercially the charm is not worth anything but the influence this primitive charm will hold over you in warding off mental vibrations is absolutely priceless".

In those days he used to sell this charm for thruppence[14] and the charm consisted of an elephant. It was quite small and quite nicely constructed. He obtained his living for many years wandering about the country, giving lectures on primitive subjects which he'd made a great study of, and selling this charm.

I asked him why he quoted this particular book, *The Martyrdom of Man* and he said that it was one of the books that he greatly cherished. He said that there were only two European books which he really cherished and that was Buckle's *Civilisation of England*[15] and this book by Winwood Reade. He admired Reade so much because he maintained that he had made a great study of many of the Occult Sciences—and it stimulated him to advise people to read it.

After the Wembley Exhibition, "The Sheik" was not seen by anybody, but it was suggested that he went to Canada. He was another character that paid great importance to his freedom.

After him, I came in contact with another character. He'd been a seaman and he'd been all over the Continent; he practised Astrology and Horoscopes on the market and he called himself "Cornelius". He wore a big black hat and a black flowing cravat and was nearly six feet tall. And the book which he was mostly on about was called *Ruins of Empire*, translated from the

14 Three pence.
15 Henry Thomas Buckle (1821-1862). His *History of Civilization in England* was published between 1857 and 1861.

French.[16] (It took me five years to find a second-hand copy; I did eventually get hold of a copy and I enjoyed it very much).

Why I was so interested in his methods of Astrology was because he paid a certain amount of importance to his own particular formulas. Now it doesn't require great intelligence to become an Astrologist, as you can buy many books on Astrology and—according to the Twelve Signs of the Zodiac— the temperament and the disposition that one is supposed to possess, according to planetary influence, has been laid down in Astrology hundreds of years ago. When you are in possession of a book on Astrology all the formulas are already there. All you have to do—it's quite simple—is to get a person's date of birth and give them a reading according to the formula of the Signs of the Zodiac. Of course, if you want to go into it from a more complicated angle, you can cast a Horoscope from the Ascending and Descending Signs. But he is the only Astrologer who I have ever met who did not conform to the formulas of Astrology, that is, the readings that were laid down hundreds of years ago. I've never met anybody apart from him who has had the courage to create his own formulas according to the conclusions that he came to individually. Through this method which he applied, which was a complete contrast to orthodox Horoscopes, he accumulated quite a number of clients, because he would give a new forecast for each three months of the year.

Unfortunately, this character was badly hurt during the air raids of the last World War and is very seldom seen about now; occasionally I go to see him.

16 I presume this is the Comte de Volney's *Ruins of Empire* (1802).

Now with Astrology and with Phrenology, and with Palmistry and Numerology and Physiognomy, the readings and the conclusions of the people who invented these Sciences have gone into formulas, and have remained so for hundreds of years. That's why I was pretty successful with my practising of Numerology, because I always told the public, "I do not give you the ancient formulas, I give you the formulas which I deduce. I give you the conclusions that I come to, and before a person can give you his own individual conclusions he must possess the powers of intuition and sense perception."

Amongst all the confusion of people leading a precarious life there were several people who had spent half of their life in an orthodox, conventional manner, then packed up this conventional way of living, and became wandering "grafters"— that is to say, they solved the problem of existence by their abilities instead of being employed by anybody.

Now, I'd reached a pitch financially where I was in a position to buy myself a gipsy caravan, which I did. With this caravan I went into the show business, and I made myself a little side-show and I travelled round to different fairs, and showed freaks of nature which I'd mostly invented myself—such as The Leopard Lady, The Angel Man, The Mermaid Monkey and the exhibition of a Cannibal, which I was supposed to have captured in the Cannibal Islands. I had this coloured gentleman with me for some considerable time; I had him inside of an iron cage and used to charge tuppence[17] to come into the show and see him, and I used to put him through a course of showing the public his ceremonial dances: how they danced at the Half-Moon; how

17 Two pence.

they danced at a wedding, and the War Dances. And we made a very comfortable living.

Now all this show life is all described in my biography which, as you know, has already been written by Mark Benney: it is called *What Rough Beast?* And I have no intentions of recording the early part of my life in my memoirs, as in my memoirs I shall concentrate on the history of interesting characters and personalities.

EARLY YEARS IN LONDON

In these past years I had wandered all over Great Britain and I had not seen London from the time I left it when I was a boy.

Now somewhere about the time when I was thirty-eight,[18] I'd sold the caravan, sold the side-show and arrived in London. I still had all the knowledge of fiddling an existence on the open road; I had no desire to achieve wealth—I only had a desire to solve the problem of existence in comfort, to meet interesting people, and to work to live and not live to work. I got myself a dilapidated room round Holborn and had enough money in my possession to keep me for some time. I explored London, mostly to see if I could find any interesting work, and also to study all the other phases of life.

I found the Caledonian Market. This market was open Tuesdays and Fridays. There were over a thousand stall-holders and there were over a thousand people selling junk on the pavement. It attracted people from all over Great Britain when they were visiting London and it also attracted an enormous amount of people who got their living from day to day by fiddling with secondhand books and antiques. I found Charing Cross Road, where all the book shops were, and went in and saw

18 Actually, Jack must have arrived in London around 1914 when he would have been thirty-three.

the book dealers and asked them if I brought books in whether they'd buy them, and what particular type of books I should look for. Well, they gave me some idea of the books that they would give me a shilling or eighteen pence or two shillings for, and I started to run around and buy books, at tuppence and thruppence apiece, which I could get a shilling and two shillings for. And there was an enormous amount of second-hand pictures in Burlington Road, Holborn, and I used to go down there every morning and see what I could find.

At this period of my life I had read so much European literature that I had no desire to read any more, and from that time up to now—which is a considerable lapse of time—I have only been interested in reading Oriental Literature. When I was wandering about the countryside I used to like reading the biographies and the memoirs of great artists and composers, the ballet dancers and theatrical people; I was always interested in any history on entertainment, and I stopped at that, so far as literature was concerned.

Then I decided to have a look at Hyde Park. I listened to the various political and religious theories the people were on about, saying what a terrible system it was we lived under—and so far as some of them were concerned, it was probably a terrible system, because unfortunately some of them had no money and they did not know how to fiddle. At this period of the history of Hyde Park, you were allowed to hold a meeting and you were allowed to sell the public a pamphlet for a penny or tuppence. I wrote a pamphlet: *How to Live on a shilling a Day and How to Get a Shilling if You Don't Have One*. This pamphlet consisted of four pages and I managed to sell it quite easily for tuppence. What I used to talk about mostly was the freedom of individuality, and

Ironfoot in 1923.

I'd explain to them the futility of wrecking yourself mentally and physically to achieve wealth, when no matter how much money you possess you can only smoke one cigarette at once, sleep in one bed at once, love one woman at once—and with all the money you possessed, which you deprived yourself your freedom to achieve, you couldn't breathe gold dust, you had to breathe fresh air the same as anybody else, and to a great extent it was an illusion.

I didn't tie any political labels of any particular kind on myself, and I had about eighteen months of this and then the authorities decided that no more literature would be allowed to be sold in the Park. It would only be allowed to be sold outside the Park, and to get the public to come outside the Park and buy a pamphlet off you for a penny or tuppence was a very complicated proposition.

I wasn't admired. I had to put up with a lot of abuse: why didn't I go to work? Why didn't I become a slave like everybody else etc?

I then decided that I'd better construct some other method of solving the problem of existence. And my argument was that if I started working, I'd only put somebody else out of work who wanted to work and I had no desire to deprive somebody of solving the problem of existence by working, when I could solve the problem of existence, so far as I was concerned, with the knowledge that I'd extracted from the aristocrats of the open road.

From there, I managed to get a basement room in Robert Street, Hampstead Road, at five shillings a week. I decided to start to turn this into a studio and use it as my consulting-room. I had a very sympathetic landlady who had a son who was a market worker—which made her a little bit more sympathetic towards me when I told her that occasionally I went on the market. I managed to scrape a few shillings together out of selling second-hand books which I found in different places, in the book shops.

I also discovered that occasionally, when I bought twenty or thirty books at tuppence or thruppence apiece, there was one book shop I used to go into where I'd put my books on the counter and the book buyer used to say: "I'll give you sixpence for this one, sixpence for this one and a shilling for this one, a shilling for this one—and for this one I'll give you ten shillings." (It was practically an impossibility to find out the real value of any second-hand book as it was difficult to get hold of any catalogues—unless you were a book dealer—giving the value of books.) I regularly went to this particular shop and the books that he didn't want off me I could always sell in another book-shop; and occasionally it happened that he'd give me a pound for a book. He wasn't concerned how much I'd bought them for, but he did appreciate the fact that I went racing and chasing about all over the place to find him particular books which he wanted.

I also went out to the markets. I made myself a beautiful Numerology board, and at that period you could go into any market in London. No licence was required; all you had to do was to give the stall-holder a shilling or two shillings. I found Petticoat Lane was very, very useful to me to pick up a few shillings, and I always found that East Lane, Walworth, was very useful too.

Then I found myself wandering about the cafés in Soho. At that period of my life I wore a silk hat and a frock-coat, which were very plentiful in those days, and which I could buy in practically any second-hand clothes shop down Petticoat Lane for three or four shillings—and I also wore a black cravat, with a silver ring and a lovely waistcoat.

And at this period of history there were several cafés in Soho and in Charlotte Street which were used by the Bohemians in London, that is to say, the characters who worked to live and didn't live to work—and also a variety of people who had other ways of fiddling an existence which were not known of to the general characters who kept themselves to the open road. In these days the main Bohemian cafés, where these people used to congregate, were The Lounge, in Gerrard Street, opposite Number Forty-Four; Mrs Merrick's Club; the dives in Queen's Court, Berwick Market; the Café Bleu and the Chat Noir, in Old Compton Street. And the two pubs where Bohemians used to congregate was the Fitzroy Tavern, in Charlotte Street, and the Marquis of Granby.

I kept my studio going in Hampstead Road, and the atmosphere was now developing into a very soothing environment. I had black velvet curtains on one wall; a tiger scene on another, some mauve cretonne curtains which I nailed tightly to the third wall—and here I hung up one or two fantastic plates and little bits of odds and ends and curios—and against the final wall I had books piled up to the ceiling. I had a small divan bed and plenty of blankets.

On the week-ends I would pop out to the suburbs of London and work my Numerology board in the markets, and on Sunday mornings I would be down Petticoat Lane. This allowed me enough money to live comfortably and also a few shillings to go around and buy books with.

All the characters at this period of history in Soho were very friendly and very interested in me.

I decided to give private lectures, and the subject of my lectures consisted of "Tramp by Circumstances", "Tramp by Desire," and "Tramp by Ambition". I described how the "tramp by circumstances" had been thrown off the industrial machine and had no desire to go back to respectability. And I described how the "tramp by desire" could have been anybody from any of the stratas of society—from the possessing class, or the middle class, or the working class—who had decided to become a tramp on account of either matrimonial trouble or financial misfortune, or else had got so frustrated that they couldn't adapt themselves to the monotonous routine of an orthodox life. And the tramps that become "tramps by ambition" very seldom remain tramps. They take it on as an experience, because it stimulates them; and this type of tramp has generally got a home or relations to go back to.

I always made it my business not to lecture about anything that anybody was an authority on or that you could read in literature. I always advocated that if you wanted to know what Aristotle or Plato or Marcus Aurelius said, go direct to the works and find out what they said.

Then I transformed my lectures—lecturing about the Law of Attitudes, the Law of Vibrations and the Law of Fascination. At this period of history, I had a considerable clientele who used to come and visit me and buy books from me. Then I listened to so many controversies about religion that I decided to create a new religion. This religion I called "Children of the Sun".

I came in contact with a lady who was very interested in Theosophy and she had friends who were also interested. And she decided that if I got premises she would give all the financial backing, and I could also get myself measured for a robe. She and all her friends were very enthusiastic about this new religion, so I had to do an enormous amount of research to extract formulas which I could read out as sermons and apply to this new religion.

I found premises in Charlotte Street, in a basement flat. This I called the Studio Temple. I found a poor artist to paint me the Twelve Signs of the Zodiac and various Occult symbols, and got some black velvet curtains to cover the walls from floor to the ceiling. I had a chair covered with black velvet, and out of a very, very thin sheet of brass I cut out the Sun. Outside of the flat, I had a sign-board painted in black and gold announcing that it was the "Headquarters of the Children of the Sun," and that Meetings would be held at 8 p.m.

I enrolled twelve members—they were all women—and I had one formula which I called a Solar Doxology. I brought into the religion only the dynamic teachings of Zoroaster, a few quotations from the *Mahabharata*, and extracted all the dynamic teaching out of the Buddhist philosophy appertaining to Karma. Unfortunately, the Law of Karma is a great subject and can be discussed from too many angles. "Karma" is extracted from Indian philosophy and it means the Law of Cause and Effect. It also means the Sequence of Activity: whatever mental and physical action you put into operation, it produces a sequence; whatever decision you make produces a sequence; doing nothing is doing something—by doing nothing you're doing something because you are taking an attitude of passive resistance.

I still have in my possession an enormous amount of literature written on the Philosophy of Karma which would be too complicated to put into my memoirs, because it's a separate subject on its own and it goes into all the details of human society. I have attempted to have it published, but every publisher I've approached with it has said that it's too complicated and too highbrow for ordinary individuals, and it will only be useful for scholars who study that particular subject. I should think in my researches I have written, in my own hand, about sixty thousand words on the Operation of Karma.

Now I am not going to bore you with this subject, but I'll just give you a slight idea of the meaning of Karma. First there is the Karma of the Individual, that is, how you act individually, mentally and physically; then there is the Karma of your Parents—and Karma of the Parents (the forefathers) has produced the situation which the individuals are born into; and there is the Mass Karma, which we are now creating, all of us, which the rising generation will be born into; and then there is the Karma of Outstanding Individuals in all kinds of thought— philosophy, ideas, inventions, productions and organizations, and all these different Karmas (that is to say, the action of the Individual, the action of the Community, the action of the Powers That Be and the reaction of Civilizations towards other Civilizations), all these different varieties of Karma produces the General State of Events.

And I got myself so acquainted with these various Laws of Karma, including the Law of Attitudes and the Science of Fascination, that I could go on for hours. I tried not to go over the same subject twice. For instance, a human being, no matter what walk of life he was in—the creature of luxury or the creature of poverty—the attitude and the decision that he makes, whether consciously or unconsciously, determines the Sequence of his Experience.

In this religion we had no Divine Power and we had no Immortality of the Soul. It was taught that when you die you decompose and you become inorganic gas, and organic gas in the ephemeral atmosphere, electrons and vibrations—and you become part of the Cosmos again. We did not teach Reincarnation and we did not teach that there is a Happy Land far, far away. We had various Rituals and I had a beautiful mauve velvet gown, which was gold-banded, and through my knowledge of White Magic, I evoked the Beneficial Vibrations from the Cosmos and dissipated the Detrimental Vibrations.

This was becoming very, very serious and the situation was becoming very, very complicated. They told their friends about it, and the place was packed to suffocation. We had a little organ there; I composed the hymns and these were not sung to a Divine Power, but they were sung to the Elements in the Cosmos.

As the months rolled on there were cars lined up in Charlotte Street and the news was going round, in all channels, how fascinating this Ritual was. The press were trying to get in to give it a write-up. We had our own secret signs so if a stranger didn't know how to give the Sign of the Children of the Sun when I opened the door to him, he didn't get in. The press did everything in their power to send someone in there to find out what was going on. The authorities couldn't get in to get any evidence of what was going on, so they couldn't issue a warrant to raid the place. It was strictly "Membership Only", and every new member had to be proposed, seconded and initiated.

I handled no money. I ordered whatever I wanted; I could order myself the most expensive books, as long as they were appertaining to Occult Cosmology, and I was living the life of luxury.

And their enthusiasm was developing to such an extent that I could see for myself that a very dangerous situation was going to occur. I knew that the authorities and the ecclesiastical organizations would not approve of a new religion which did not recognize a Divine Power and advocated that it was possible—quite possible—to be the architect of your own destiny individually. It wasn't possible to be the architect of your destiny physically, but it was possible to be the architect of your destiny mentally; and your temperament and your capabilities and the decisions that you came to about life belonged to you and you alone, and there was no necessity to accept the dogmas and theories which had been handed down by heredity and tradition.

I closed the premises because I was convinced that instead of society being sympathetic towards this new religion and being willing to find out what it was all about and going into its new doctrines and its new philosophy, it would have been denounced to such an extent that I would have got classified as a very, very eccentric character. And I was not prepared to take these responsibilities on my shoulders, not at this period of my life.

However, while it lasted it was a very satisfying experience. It was one of the most delightful experiences of my life, because I had semi-economic security. I didn't have to go out and face the public and make a clown of myself in order to get the necessities of life, and it gave me plenty of time for research into the subjects which I wished to study and perhaps someday some scholars might appreciate the manuscripts which I wrote during this period of my life. I have all these manuscripts, which I could not write to-day, and could not have written at any other period of my life, as at that period of my life I had leisure and complete economic security—everything I wanted. I didn't desire the things that weren't necessary to life, but everything I desired was bought for me by this very sincere community who operated this religion with loyalty and sincere co-operation.

I often wondered: supposing I had carried on the Children of the Sun? There were other curious and weird and mysterious societies operating in different parts of London who had constructed a particular type of philosophy. The main philosophy which I reincarnated into the sermons of the Children of the Sun was mainly taken from the Buddhist Catechism and also the *Rubaiyat* of Omar Khayyam. And some of the main verses which I took out of the *Rubaiyat* were:

> And that inverted Bowl we call the Sky:
> Whereunder crawling coop't we live and die,
> Lift not Thy hands to It for help—for It
> Rolls impotently on as Thou or I.

> Ah love! Could Thou and I with Fate conspire
> To grasp this sorry Scheme of Things entire,
> Would not we shatter it to bits—and then
> Re-mould it nearer to the Heart's Desire

> Alike for those who for To-day prepare
> And those that after a Tomorrow stare
> A Muezzin from the Tower of Darkness cries
> 'Fools! Your Reward is neither Here nor There!'

However, that was the end of the Children of the Sun. The Ritual was given to the Elements and the place was closed up for the month and I turned it into the School of Magic.

Different lectures on different subjects were given at various parts of the week, and the entrance was free. I changed a good bit of the scenery, and with a few pounds that I had left I went round and collected all the cheap, interesting books which I could lay my hands on and started building a library.

However, I was now free and out came my Numerology board again, and I thought of constructing a fascinating method of giving a Forecast of Events, so I constructed a new board on which I fastened twenty-five cards, and I call this "Take a Pick". I went out to the markets and experimented with this. I held a pack of cards in my hand and then one of the audience could take a card and whatever number was on that card they got a reading from Numerology which was a forecast of what precautions to take to the coming events of the next three months. It was very successful but it caused too much of a crowd, and I also found it difficult to operate it in many markets on account of the cards, so I destroyed the board and wandered about from market to market with my original Astrology board.

While all this was going on, Soho and the West End were very interesting. I knew all the important orators in Hyde Park and when I used to meet them they used to inform me where a lecture was being held, and what it was all about. Bonar Thompson, a Hyde Park orator, was giving lectures once a week on different subjects in The Lounge, Gerrard Street; at this period there were lectures being given at the Forum Club in Gerrard Street on Sociology; Charlie Burns was giving lectures on the modus operandi of production, and there was another character called Jenner, who was a free-thinker, and obtained his living giving lectures in Hyde Park and tearing paper for theatre queues. I always remember the opening of his lectures, when he would say: "It is not necessary to make a Hell of this world in order to achieve Paradise in the next."

At this period of history there were some very brilliant speakers in Hyde Park and there were also plenty of maniacs talking a lot of tripe.

In the first place, there were at least three thousand characters floating about in and out of the West End and backwards and forwards to the Caledonian Market buying, for a few coppers, anything they could get hold of, such as second-hand books, little bits of decorative china, curios, oil paintings (if they were cheap); fans were very popular because there were a lot of artistic people who liked to nail fans on the wall—and there were all kinds of fiddling commodities that could be bought in Houndsditch. Some of these characters were pretty clever and had a great knowledge of books, and some of them had quite a good knowledge of antiques. However, they all fiddled a more or less comfortable existence and they all had the same attitude that they only required the essential necessities of life. And they also used to mingle with the Bohemians and consider themselves Bohemians.

Sitting in various cafés in the early hours of the morning in those days was profitable because the film people used to come round and they used to collect characters for crowd work. On several occasions I did a little bit of crowd work; I was in one picture—but I never saw it shown over here—called *While London Sleeps* and it was taken in Trafalgar Square, at about three o'clock in the morning. I had a small part to play: I had to lead the crowd behind me up to the front of Nelson's Column to listen to the speaker.

During this period I was most conscious of the fact of "what am I going to do when this particular method of solving the problem of existence is played out?" So I trained myself to do monologues. One of the monologues I used to do was entitled "The Dying Hobo"—this monologue everybody seemed to like, and it was another card up my sleeve for raising a few bob:

> Beside a western water-tank one cold December day,
> Inside of a car-box a dying hobo lay;
> His partner stood beside him with low bowed
> down head,
> Listening to the last words that the dying hobo said:
> 'I'm going to a Better Land where everything is bright,
> Where hand-outs go on wishes and you can camp out
> every night;
> You never have to work at all and never darn your socks,
> And little drops of whiskey come travelling down the
> rocks
> Tell all the boys in 'Frisco for me in their eyes no tears
> should dwell,
> I'm going to a Better Land where they hate the name
> called 'work'!
> Hark! I hear a whistle! I must catch her on the fly,
> One more beautiful hand-out I'd like before I die…'
> His head rolled back. He'd sang his last refrain.
> His partner took his hat and shoes and caught the east
> bound train.[19]

19 This is Jack's version of a traditional folk-song based on the 19th century poem "Bingen on the Rhine" by Caroline Norton (1808–1877).

I also had a little bit of comedy patter which I could put over:

"When I first came to London I said to a copper, 'How can I get to Piccadilly?' And he said, 'Get a 29 bus.' So I counted twenty-nine buses and when the twenty-ninth bus came up I said to the conductor, 'Does this go to Piccadilly?' And he said, 'No.' 'Well,' I said, 'it's got Piccadilly on the outside of it.' He said, 'I know it has—it's got Nestle's Milk on the other side of it, but it doesn't go to Switzerland; you want a train.'

So I went to the railway station and I said to the porter, 'Can I get a train here?' And he said, 'No, they belong to the Railway Company.'

So then I walked round the railway station and I saw the Station Manager, and I said to him, 'How long will the next train be?' And he said, 'An engine and forty carriages.'

This nonsense I used to put over in different night clubs which had a cabaret, and it went over very well. I even do it now sometimes when I'm asked, and during the first Soho Festival, which was 1956, I performed it on a stage in Golden Square.

Now the other people who were floating around the cafés, which considered themselves Bohemian cafés, were part-time actors, part-time film workers who did crowd work, artists' models, people who were running round composing various articles about events, and poor artists who could get an existence by flogging their paintings cheaply to tourists. The poor artists didn't have too bad a time because there was plenty of work in decorating clubs and doing murals on the walls. A great percentage of these people had their basements or cellars round Charlotte Street and Bloomsbury, which they called their "studios," and they were always willing, providing the character was in the Bohemian circle, to put somebody up for the night. And there was another group of people who were part of this great Bohemian circle who organized the Sun Bathers Group; in the summer-time they used to sun-bathe at the Welsh Harp, Hendon. Quite a number of them had sleeping-bags and they used to go down to the River Lea and camp down there.

The Caledonian Market produced an existence for a great many as they could raise a few bob helping a stall-holder for a day. The Caledonian Market was the greatest clutter market in Europe, and you could always fiddle enough to eat. You could buy something, if you had some idea of value, for a few coppers off of the ground out in the junk dealers department, and you could take it over to the other side of the market, where the antique dealers were, and you could sell an article, that perhaps you had bought for a shilling, for five or six bob.

The real antique dealers over in this department weren't concerned what you'd paid for it—they would give you a fair profit for it providing they were convinced that they could also sell it for a fair profit. Hundreds of these dealers, who got their living with the clutter, bought all kinds of Oriental pots and vases, and brass and copper. Many of them didn't really know anything about antiques. If you got hold of an Oriental vase the character who sold it to you, who was obtaining his living by selling clutter, he would only know that the vase was Oriental—Chinese or Indian—but he would not know whether it was *glissone*, Cantonese, *famille verte*, *famille rose* or Nankin. So you had to know yourself, you had to have some idea of value.

If the character had a print, he wouldn't know whether it was a Medici print, a Baxter print, or a Bertolozzi, and all he knew was that it was a print. There were quite a lot of black and white Hogarth prints floating about; there were quite a lot of early medical books too, all the great poets were up there for thruppence; the memoirs of actors and actresses; period lace; curios of all descriptions...The Caledonian Market always holds sweet memories for me, because it provided many of the little fiddles I used to do in order to solve the problem of existence. It assisted in keeping me for years, and many others too. I can say the Caledonian Market assisted me to get a living for a good twenty years.

I used to look for mounted cameos and intaglios, curios in wood carving and mounts and the ivory handles of walking sticks. Sometimes I'd buy strings of Venetian beads and with rolled gold wire, which I used to get at Massey and Johnsons, I used to turn Venetian beads into drop ear-rings with hooks for the pierced ears. This art of wire-working I learned from the wire-workers when I was on the open road. In the whole of the Caledonian Market there were only two professional wire-workers who obtained their living by making ear-rings and bangles out of rolled gold wire—even they used to buy off me.

Another fiddle I started was buying cut-glass perfume bottles, which I could get for tuppence or thruppence apiece, and blending a perfume with eau-de-cologne. I always had a bottle of perfume—a nice cut-glass bottle of perfume—in my pocket when I was walking around, for many people used to ask me if I had some perfume. What sold them was the cut-glass bottle; some were very decorative: I even used small decanters, if they were cut-glass, which were lying about junk stores, and I'd tie a bit of ribbon about them. I also knew a place where I could get decorative perfume bottle labels to stick on them.

I went to the library and I studied the history of cameos. When I bought a cameo for two or three shillings, the person who sold me it would not know whether it was an historical cameo, whether it was a classical cameo, or whether it was a commercial cameo. All they knew was that it was a cameo. Of course, it was not possible to buy quantities of cameos, you could just accidentally come across them here and there—and you could only come across intaglios occasionally. The onyx and cornelian and agate intaglios which had somebody's initials on were practically useless. The only intaglios that were any good were the ones which had the Coat of Arms of aristocratic heraldry. All these intaglios had been pulled out of seals at some time or other, and the cameos had been pulled out of old frames. These I had no trouble in selling in Poland Street, to Calipe and Dentons. They specialized in buying loose stones, every stone known in the world. They'd buy loose stones and they'd buy coral necklaces, and little pieces of broken jade. And I had another place where they would buy broken ivory figures which were eventually re-carved again in some kind of a design. Loose stones—amethysts, topazes, garnets, white sapphires, jargoons, carbuncles—they all had their trade value to Calipe and Dentons, and jewellers from all over Great Britain used to go there to buy the loose stones they required for mounting into various types of jewellery.

This knowledge I kept to myself because I used to spend quite a while in the suburbs of London, looking round clutter shops to see what I could see.

There was also some characters who got part-time jobs at Covent Garden Market; there were others that got part-time jobs down at the docks for one night; and there were plenty of part-time jobs washing dishes in cafés, restaurants and clubs.

And with these fiddling abilities this great crowd of Bohemians could survive and have their freedom. Round about this period Scott-Moncrieff wrote a book entitled *Café Bar*.[20] He put me into the book under a fictitious name; he called me "Professor McCurio," and my photograph was on the paper cover of the book.

During this period there was tremendous activity which made living easy. People were moving about and coming and going; new cafés and old ones being rebuilt, re-decorated; thousands upon thousands of tourists in and out of Soho from the suburbs, from the south of England, from the north of England, the Midlands, Scotland and Wales; from all the cities. The money poured into the cafés and some of it found its way into the pockets of the Bohemians. Almost anybody with any artistic ability could get a part-time job. If you were a bit short yourself then one of your friends was sure to be a bit luckier at the time and, perhaps, having moved into his studio, wanted you to give him a hand. It was easy to live because there was a brotherhood unlike anywhere else on earth.

And any butcher would give you some odds and ends of meat for fourpence and with a loaf and a few vegetables you could make a banquet for three or four people that would cost, between them, three or four shillings to dine. And you very seldom saw Bohemians shabby because you could also go to the

---

20 George Scott-Moncrieff (1910–1974) *Café Bar: A Novel Without Hero or Plot*. London: Wishart, 1932.

Caledonian Market and for thirty shillings you could get clothes that made you look like a character just out of the Chamber of Commerce. No Bohemian allowed himself to be scruffy then. Also it was quite easy to get a basement or a cellar for seven or eight shillings a week.

I remember a girl who called herself "The White Butterfly" and her studio was in a cellar, with bare bricks all hung with black curtains (black curtains were very popular amongst Bohemians; they were easy to get and easy to make— anything dyed black can look effective). At the end of the room she had a stage with a huge frame around it and she used to do artistic posing for her friends there, which a pure-minded person could not take exception to. She used to do the "Dance of the Seven Veils", the "Dances of Psyche Before the Bath" and "Psyche After the Bath", and "I've Got My Eye on You", and she was also a model at various art schools. She was seen around, in and about the Bohemian cafés, and had many friends in the circle at this time. Eventually she fell in love with an artist and they went to Montparnasse, in Paris. I remember bidding them goodbye.

There was another character and we used to call him "Ironface." He had a cellar, too, and he used to work a dodge with cheap pearls. I visited his studio and he had a fantastic chariot race round the walls in plaster of Paris, which he had constructed himself—and he was not a sculptor, he had no training, and yet this peculiar design which he had put on the walls was quite effective. Now, when cheap rows of pearls came out, he used to buy them for about fourpence a row, and he used to get around about Cambridge Circus when the theatres came out and he'd go up to a woman and say, "Pardon me, Miss or Madame, but you've just dropped your pearls out of your handbag." And it was very seldom that the woman would say "No" or "You must be mistaken" or tell him to go away—they used to say: "Thank you very much," and give him three or four shillings to buy cigarettes with. He had to have terrific nerve to accomplish this feat, and he didn't have any competition.

He was a great arguer and he was always in arguments and discussions about Hegelian philosophy; Hegel was his idol.

Then there was the White Yogi's studio in a basement in Old Compton Street, and he called it "The World Upside Down," and that was about right. Over the whole of the ceiling he had a wire netting with grass sacking attached to it, the sort of stuff that costers use with their barrows for fruit, and down into the room were artificial flowers and fruit in brilliant colours, upside down. The floor was covered with mirrors with clouds painted on them. He had a flood-lit statue of a goddess in white marble, and he used to do private crystal readings down here. When he sat down to give a reading, he wore an Oriental dressing-gown with dragons on it. The place was quite nice to sit in because he had, in the summer-time, three electric fans he could turn on. He also used to write articles on Occult subjects for a colonial publication. Apart from that, he came from quite a good family and had an income of about thirty shillings a week so he had nothing to worry about. He was quite acquainted with the Philosophy of Karma and later on, when I opened the School of Wisdom in New Oxford Street, he was often there. He did his readings squatting on a carpet on the floor and he had a sofa, where his clients sat, which was covered with a beautiful oriental gold bedspread. He had a little Buddha in a corner in a shrine with incense burning to it.

Many people tried to get into discussions with him but he was a quiet character and had no desire to discuss with anybody. All he would say is that if things are because they are, they can't be anything else than what they are; and as long as you're solving the problem of existence, why worry? He was listening to some characters arguing about the system one day and he said, "Well, if you don't like the system you live under, why don't you alter it—it's your system, not mine; although I live under it I'm not of it: I'm entirely apart from it."

He also occasionally used to walk round the Caledonian Market giving cards away, privately advertising himself. The premises in Old Compton Street which he lived under was bombed during the last World War.

There was another character whom we used to call "The Highwayman," and he had an art of solving the problem of existence which was his own invention—and it was very ingenious. He had a cellar in Allen Street and I went down there for a cup of tea and a chat, and he had boxes of dilapidated wills, solicitors' wills, parchment wills, and he also had boxes of dilapidated period tapestry which he'd collected in the Caledonian Market and off of furniture in rag stores. He also had another box with several pairs of dilapidated gloves, and then he had a few yards of lace ribbon and a quantity of small picture frames about two feet long and two feet wide. On the wall there were several pictures and inside of these pictures there were gloves with tapestry and lace on—gauntlets, with the tapestry turned into highwayman's gauntlets, and with a bit of lace put on them; they were placed on top of the parchment and then they were framed. He used any kind of a frame, providing it was the right size, and they looked very effective because the tapestry was early Victorian (some of it might have been earlier) and all the words were written in old English on the parchment. And he used to come round with these picture frames with these gloves and he used to flog them in cafés. And they looked very, very effective; several of these peculiar Highwayman's pictures were hung up in different clubs in the West End. He also had one or two dealers who bought them off him in the Caledonian Market and managed to sell them again. It was his own original idea and he had no competition.

And there was George—he was called "George the Penman." In some period of his life he'd been a solicitor's clerk and he used to wear old-fashioned clothes and had side-boards like Lord Byron. He had a cellar in Tottenham Street; it was decorated with blue cretonne curtains round the wall and on pieces of cardboard he'd got an artist to paint him various mysterious pentagrams, which he constructed himself. He was called "George the Penman" because he used to write letters for people; he had a very fine collection of books on law, and his main hobby was studying them. And he was a very, very useful character to know for a lot of people in the West End when they got into various controversies with the authorities. He had a small income left him, about a pound a week, from an aunt, so in this period of the history of the West End he had nothing to worry about.

There was a beautiful Chinese woman who solved the problem of existence by fortune-telling in Berwick Market. Her studio was at the back of Robert Street, and it was a beautiful studio because it was all in Oriental style. She had some very nice "Oriental Madonnas" painted on silk. She was a clairvoyant and she compiled fifty-two different readings; her method of telling fortunes was this: she had fifty-two joss sticks with numbers on them and you picked one out of a brass vase and she handed you your reading from the number which was on the joss stick. But she only used to come out on Saturday—through the week she used to do part-time posing at different art schools.

And then there was the famous Epstein model, Delores.[21] She was a very good friend of mine and was often round at my studio with her friends as my guest. And she also had a cellar underneath the Sunshine Café in Carnaby Street. (This cafe opened at twelve o'clock at night and shut at six o'clock in the morning. At that period it relied on people who went to a dance hall over the road and who used to come in for their breakfast. It used to be visited by the Bohemians in the West End as well; they would sit in the café every night, fantastically dressed, holding court.) She was very interested in going to debates and discussions and I often saw her at the Scholars Society which met in Tottenham Court Road on Sunday nights. Everybody loved Delores. She never used to say a lot but she always carried that sympathetic smile. She had a curious hobby of collecting weird dolls made out of *papier mache*, though it didn't matter if they had wooden heads as long as they looked something like period dolls, and she dressed them in the national costumes of different continental countries. And at this period of her life I had a friend who was a barrister and I took him round one night to the Sunshine Café in Carnaby Street and he got very friendly with Delores and that was the last I saw of her. Later I heard that she'd gone with the wind and I was very sorry. I should think Delores was in and out of my company for about six years.

21 Real name Norine Fournier Lattimore (née Schofield), 1894–1934. She first modelled for Jacob Epstein in 1921.

And up above her lived Percy Brownfield who, in the early part of his career, had been working in a bank and inherited a little bit of money; he obtained his living by his own ingenious idea—he used to cut the reproductions of oil paintings out of *The Connoisseur*, an antique journal which you could buy for thruppence or fourpence second-hand. It would have three or four beautiful coloured prints of famous oil paintings, and these he used to glue onto the back of a potato sack and then put them in any cheap frame he could get hold of. At that time you could buy frames at the Caledonian Market for tuppence or thruppence. And he had some secret ingredients of his own which he mixed with varnish and he gave these prints two coats of this varnish, and when they were dry they did look very effective. These he had no trouble in selling for two or three shillings apiece to different characters who were decorating their studios.

Then there was a character who we used to call "Rubber," and he invented a very ingenious way of solving the problem of existence. He got an artist who was a sign-writer to cut him out a rubber stamp and on this were the words "Banned From the Public Library." And he would go up the Caledonian Market and he would buy some novels at tuppence or thruppence apiece, and then he would get a postcard of a nude model and he'd stick that in the front of the cover of the book, and then he'd stamp the book all over with "Banned From the Public Library." And he had no trouble in selling these books quietly in and out of the cafés and the clubs to different tourists. He lived under the Arches in Camden Town in a home-made caravan, and by this method of solving the problem of existence he lived a very comfortable life for many years because he had no trouble in selling at least three to four books a day. If you had an income of ten shillings a day, in those days, a Bohemian could live like a lord—providing you cooked your own banquets. A bit of rice, a pound of onions and four penn'orth[22] of meat in a butcher's shop—which the Bohemians used to call "block ornaments"—and you had a banquet. He joined the Sun Bathers and in the summer-time he used to spend most of his days sun-bathing, and at night time he'd be running around flogging these novels stamped "Banned From the Public Library."

There was a pavement artist who had a cellar underneath The Seven Dials and he used to do two pictures on the pavement in chalk, one of "The Laughing Cavalier," and the other one of "The Madonna." I went down to his den in The Dials and had a cup of tea with him, and the walls of his studio were covered with small oil paintings which he'd done. These oil paintings—he had quite a quantity of them—he used to sell in the winter-time to art dealers who were interested in ecclesiastical subjects. I asked him one day who his favourite artist was (he was well acquainted with art) and he said he was very fond of George Morland, and he said, "because George Morland[23] was a tramp, a vagabond and a Bohemian." Later on I managed to get a copy of the memoirs of George Morland and I enjoyed them very much, and recommended the book to many young artists to read.[24]

He would occasionally come into the cafés and if he liked a character he would do a quick sketch of them and give

22 Four pennies worth.
23 George Morland (1763–1804) a painter of rustic scenes and animals.
24 *Memoirs of the Life of the Late George Morland* (ed. John Hassell). London: James Cundee, 1806.

them the sketch free of charge. He never charged for any of the sketches he did in the cafés; he wouldn't sell a sketch, he would give it to you for nothing. His "Laughing Cavalier," which he used to do on the pavement, used to cause him to get quite a nice crowd. One of his pitches on Sunday night was around by the Art Gallery in Trafalgar Square. In his early days he had been to Paris and he had been to art schools, and most of his friends were buskers and people who used to entertain theatre queues.

In these days from the top of Fitzroy Square down to Rainbow Corner, Piccadilly, in and out the side streets there were about three hundred different cafés and there were also about three hundred different types of night clubs. The history of the underworld and the racketeering that went on in these days was written in a book called *Madness After Midnight*, by Jack Glicco.[25] There's a photograph of me in the book and there's also a nice article about me. Another book which was very popular amongst the Bohemians in these days was written by a playwright by the name of Lionel Britton. It was an auto-biography and it was called *Hunger and Love*.[26] Both these books are worth reading. Another important book which is well worth reading is a book entitled *Half My Days and Nights*, by Hubert Nicholson.[27] It has a brief history of the Coffee An'[28]; I am mentioned on many pages.

There was another character known as "Caravan Holmes." He was an explorer in his early days and he contracted some

25 London: Elek Books, 1952.
26 Lionel Britton (1887–1971). *Hunger and Love*. London & New York: Putnam, 1931.
27 Sub-titled *Autobiography of a Reporter*. London: William Heinemann Ltd, 1941.
28 A Bohemian café in Soho where Jack first met Nicholson.

kind of fever while he was exploring which unfortunately caused him to be unable to walk—he was given a bath chair by Bernard Shaw. He ran a journal at one time and it was called *Bold Views*. It was flogged in the West End and Soho for thruppence and the material it consisted of was mostly about what was going on between personalities and characters in the West End. I wrote several articles in this magazine. He also wrote a book in which he mentions me but the book is mostly about his travels in different parts of the world; the book is called *A Candle at Both Ends*.[29]

A lot was talked and a lot was written about the vice in Bohemia. That's why some of the people went there, hoping to see something a bit out of the ordinary. But generally they were disappointed—at least as far as the Bohemians were concerned. The Bohemian isn't immoral, he's just got a different morality. He's generous, good to his friends, a lover of life and the Arts. He doesn't look for a wife but for an Ideal. He's a man of experience but, with all his experience, it's not sex he's after, but companionship. Real love is the companionship that you derive from a woman and the companionship which you give her. And when you do find a woman like this, or a woman finds a man like that, it's not important what their personality is or what their physique is like. If couples were to cherish each other's companionship a bit more then they would get more harmony. And the Bohemian knows that if two people of the opposite sex can establish mental and physical harmony all the problems of the world are as nothing.

29 I think Jack must mean *My Candle at Both Ends* by John Carveth Wells, London: Jarrolds, 1943.

Perhaps a man and a woman would live together for a few months or years and then separate to continue their search for the Ideal. If they parted there were never any hard feelings—the next day might find them sitting in the same café, discussing the same old subjects.

There were plenty of clubs shut down and police raids were common enough, but usually the offences were nothing more than selling drinks after hours or permitting gambling on the premises. Or perhaps the owner had a run of bad luck and there were a few too many fights.

During this period, in August I always went to the Isle of Wight for the August season. I used to join the gipsies and camp out in a sleeping bag. There I worked my Numerology board on the Promenade when the carnivals were on. At the sea-side places on the Isle of Wight—Ryde, Ventnor, Shanklin, Newport and Cowes—you were only allowed to get your living when the carnivals were on. All I had to do was to fiddle enough money to buy food and cigarettes. The rest was freedom—I had a wonderful time. On Sunday I used to cross over to Portsmouth, in front of the War Memorial, and work the Promenade at Southsea. This piece of ground was considered to be 'No Man's Land', but eventually the Portsmouth and Southsea Corporation put a stop to this.

CLUBS, CAFÉS AND CHARACTERS

Now a lot of people think that the first School of Wisdom opened in New Oxford Street. As a matter of fact, it did not: it opened for eight months in a basement in a court off Tottenham Court Road in Goodge Street. The rent was very cheap and I managed to buy, in the Caledonian Market, very cheap, some stage scenery canvas which came in very useful to hang up on the wall. There was a lot of Hyde Park orators came to see me, and any of their crowd could come down there. They could buy a loaf, and something to go with it, and make their own sandwiches, or go out and buy fish and chips, and sit down there and eat them. It was open till four or five o'clock in the morning.

I had nothing to worry about at this period, because I was doing a mail order business; I was giving readings through the post. I composed the pamphlets describing why it would be an asset for you to have a reading and I distributed this pamphlet when I went out into the suburbs with my Numerology board. And I had about thirty shillings a week coming in through the post, so I didn't have to go out so much and jump about.

When this School of Wisdom at Goodge Street was set up, I notified most of my friends (but not everybody) and some of the Hyde Park orators used to bring their friends from the

Park and we mostly used to talk and have some discussions—there were no lectures given here—and there were couple of buskers used to come down with a banjo and a mandolin. And everything was going along nicely until a journalist happened to get in there one night, and he wrote an article in *The Evening Standard* about me and also about this school of wisdom, and how Bohemians, Hyde Park orators and gipsies congregated there to have little talks and discussions. It was quite a good article but it caused the wrong vibrations. The address of the place was in the article and the next day I was invaded by sightseers and people who wanted to amuse themselves by looking at what they considered 'peculiar people'—Bohemians: there was one or two young fellows with beards and there was one or two young artists with their hair on their shoulders and there was several pretty models down there wearing sandals and artistic skirts. And I found that night after night I couldn't cope with the people who wanted to invade the place.

However, there was a character who was very friendly with me. Although he led an orthodox and conventional life he was also very fond of being in the company of Bohemians, and he had a friend who was an estate agent—and when I told him about the situation he said, "I've got just the place for you in New Oxford Street." And I took the premises, which were quite a nice size, and the rent was fifteen shillings a week. I soon collected a few of the poor artists and between us we put some fantastic murals on the wall, and got some orange boxes and covered them with lino and then made cushions out of rags, drew some weird pentagrams and designs on the wall, and put the Twelve Signs of the Zodiac on the ceiling. Then I contacted friends who had a little bit of influence and drew up a pamphlet.

And this is what the pamphlet said:

A LEAFLET ANNOUNCING THE OPENING OF A SCHOOL OF WISDOM AT
89, NEW OXFORD STREET:

The object of the School is to hold Private Lectures, Socials and Discussions concerning existing Phenomena, including Mathematics, Economics, Evolution, Philosophy, Sociology, Anthropology, Mohammed, Bramah, Confucius, Zoroastra, Yogi, Foundations of Superstition, Phrenology, Graphology, Numerology, Art in all its Manifestations and all Subjects which have a bearing on the Human Mind including Environment.

I did not live on these premises as I had my studio in Robert Street, Hampstead Road which I never gave up. I kept it going for twenty years even if I was away out of London for a month or two months.

There was nobody allowed to become a member of this School unless they were proposed and seconded; we also had our secret sign, which was given at the door. The School ran for two and a half years, and luckily it was not everybody that got to know about it.

This School had a great many theories attached to it and it also had people who were members who were qualified authorities on different subjects. While it lasted its members were very sincere and fortunately during its operation it did not get a write-up of any description. Its lectures, debates and discussions were supported by collections from its members, and it accumulated a wonderful library, partly from what I contributed and partly what was contributed by its members. There was nobody actually employed; the members took turns in running the catering side of it which only consisted of sandwiches and cakes and mineral waters. It was a meeting-place, it wasn't run for any financial motive; the whole set-up belonged to its members and it was the members who ran it. Although I established and organized it, it did not belong to me—it was just a meeting-place where we could meet one another and have discussions and debates. It was visited by members' friends and when it was serious, it was really serious, and when it had its social sides to it, it was very enjoyable. It attracted a good many scholars in London who were really very seriously interested in studying Occult subjects and also studying Oriental Philosophy, and there were one or two characters who studied giving readings and who later practised Astrology and Clairvoyance. It had no political motives at all, although on many occasions there were lectures on Sociology and Psychology.

It had almost every one of the books in the "Thinkers Library",[30] and it also had a colossal library appertaining to the Occult subjects. It also had about thirty-two books on Buddhism and other subjects mentioned on the programme. They were all used and well borrowed.

All the lectures that were given here were unusual. There were even lectures that you couldn't hear in Hyde Park; you certainly couldn't hear the peculiar theories that were discussed in any political meeting. And they would attempt to get down

30 A series of 140 hardback books published by Watts & Co., London between 1929 and 1951 featuring essays by H. G. Wells, Charles Darwin, Herbert Spencer and many others.

to the rock bottom of the Cause of Cause, and we got ourselves into such a turmoil that it was very hard to believe that whatever Cause existed—no matter what it was, whether it was supposed to be a Divine Cause or any Cause—it must have had a Cause before it could have existed. And although the members of the School of Wisdom didn't tie any political labels on themselves, they did advocate a better system of society.

And eventually, after it had operated for about two and a half years, it collapsed: the lease ran out and I decided to give myself a couple of years freedom, because there was plenty of places I could go to stimulate myself and meet different characters.

After the School of Wisdom closed about five or six private Occult Schools were opened—by members who had obtained their learning from the School of Wisdom. But they weren't called "School of Wisdom" although they took the same idea, and the same constructive policy with them, and the same formulas. There was one place which called itself "The Tibetan School of Wisdom" and that was operated somewhere round Notting Hill Gate by one of the members of the School, and there was a temple opened in Kensington called the "School of Karma"—which was also opened by one of the members of the School. But these new places did not attract any of our crowd because they were too far away. Then there was one member of the School of Wisdom who opened a private studio in Richmond; he called his place "The Mauve Circle", but he attracted his own clientele to it. But all these different schools that opened up afterwards, in different parts of London, had nothing at all to do with the activities of the Bohemians of Soho and the West End. I've seen a couple of characters in the last few years and they're operating very successfully, but on a financial basis; their operations are a business and their object is mercenary as well as accumulating as much obscure learning as possible. With ours, the main object was to secure obscure learning not obtainable in any public library; it was not our motive to discuss ordinary academic subjects that were discussed generally—we wanted to branch off into a different channel.

After the School of Wisdom I met Jinny, my wife. She suited me because she had travelled about with a circus and had been a ballet dancer and a trapeze artist, and she had also been a model. We got married by a special licence and she remained with me for twenty-five years. She is now gone with the wind— she died in Birmingham about eight years ago. We had a very good companionship because she was very interested in Music, Literature, Art and Philosophy. I used to take her away with me in the summer-time and in the winter she used to like to do a bit of posing for the art schools. Occasionally she would co-operate with some show people on a fair ground in London in the summer-time.

It was about two years before I operated anything else. Round about this period The Lounge, in Gerrard Street, had collapsed; the lease had run out, so that was another Bohemian rendezvous gone with the wind. And then the Chat Noir—closed—that was another one! Then just about next door in Old Compton Street, to where the "White Yogi" used to have his studio, there was a cellar opened by an artist and it was called "Peggy's Cellar," and that remained a meeting-place for about a year. And then the Café Bleu changed hands and it was all redecorated and reorganized and it ceased to cater for Bohemians anymore; it started catering mostly for theatre-goers, at night.

During this lapse I was getting a living by going to the Caledonian Market; at this period I started fiddling about with junk myself. I had a stall with mostly bric-a-brac on it and junk, and I used to buy my own junk up there and put it on my own stall and sell it again. I was up there Tuesdays and Fridays right the year round, apart from going away in August for a month. During this time there was a General Strike and an enormous amount of poverty and struggle and many down-and-outs, and even a lot of Bohemians found that they had to become respectable in order to survive.[31]

Things got very, very quiet, and I was sitting in Peggy's Cellar when a character asked me why didn't I open a place, and I said, "Well, if you can find some cheap premises, I might have a go." That August I'd had a pretty good season on the Isle of Wight.

So he managed to get me some premises in Greek Street. I had no trouble in getting a few characters around me to co-operate, so we decided—I don't know why—to call this place "The Albatross." We got some of the poor artists to put some fantastic designs on the walls; I had plenty of velvet and cretonne curtains and scenery that was left over from my other places and I got these up. At the end of this studio coffee-house I put a tiger on one wall, and a giraffe on the other wall, and I got some old carpets and mats and put them on the floor, painted the floor black, and got some timber and made little settees and divans. In the School of Wisdom I could accommodate fifty people comfortably, but in this place, in Greek Street, I could get a hundred and fifty in quite comfortably. It was impossible to run it as an exclusive place or have it for anything serious, because it was right in the heart of Soho. However, we

31 Presumably 1926. The 9-day General Strike lasted from May 4–13.

got some buskers and their guitars and we opened and went into full swing.

And a fortnight after the Café Bleu and the Chat Noir had collapsed, I was packed to suffocation. So I made it my business to take the names and addresses of at least two thousand people whom I knew in case I wanted to use them at any time.

Although the Caledonian Market was still operating, all the fiddlers were having a rather tough time of it. There was a proper lull in the West End after the General Strike, things were very quiet and everybody seemed to be struggling to survive. Anyway, I got this Bohemian crowd going in The Albatross; luckily it was just paying its expenses and covering its liabilities, and I put on as many staff as I possibly could. The staff consisted of any of our crowd who wanted part-time work. (At that time many Bohemians had emigrated to Paris. Somebody had got organised in Montparnasse.) We had quite a few talented buskers that used to perform every night. We had a character who could recite "The Shooting of Dan McGrew," and "The Green Eye of the Little Yellow God" and another who could sing "Danny Boy". There was also a young lady who could play a violin—classical music—very, very beautifully.

There was no trouble in the place at all. The only trouble was that it became so crowded that I had to shut it down for a month. Then I decided to re-open and then I had to shut it down again. At this time there was nowhere where the Bohemians could go. Some of them used to go into "Number Four", Old Compton Street, but that was only a small café. There was a little turning at the side of Greek Street where there was a little coffee-house called "The Sunshine". It was open all night and they served a very, very good bowl of soup for fourpence and a terrific amount of bread pudding for tuppence. While the place lasted it did very well. Things were getting rather complicated for me, however, because I had to keep on closing my place down. It got packed to suffocation, and I had to keep on turning people away. (It was never raided by the authorities, but there's no doubt the authorities gave a good look at it to see what was going on.)

Eventually I sold it for a few pounds, because I was actually glad to get out of it. It was impossible to operate: there was such a flood of people who had heard about it and wanted to get in, it just got beyond me, I couldn't cope with it. I was quite happy operating a place which held about fifty people but not a hundred and fifty people and then on top of that another hundred and fifty people trying to get in. There was nothing I could do about it, so I took out my scenery and went down to Cornwall.

I went to St Ives for a month, and I thought to myself: "Down here I can just about recuperate." I took my little Jinny with me. It was September and we had a lovely month of sunshine and recreation there at the end of the season.

Then we came back to London. I wasn't interested in operating any more places, not for a bit. I packed up my clutter stall in the Market, and instead of having that I was satisfied with fiddling about with odds and ends to the trade. Then I met an Indian who was a Palmist; he'd just come back from the sea-side and he'd accumulated a little bit of capital and he decided to open an Oriental Bazaar. We found premises in Brixton. He had quite a number of Indian friends who allowed him to have a little of their Oriental commodities, brassware and silkware, on sale or return, and also a few reproduction carpets. And for that period I assisted him with his Bazaar, but I wasn't at the Bazaar all day, because you can't imagine my being at any place

ISSUES
20 GLEN AVE.
OAKLAND CA 94611
510-652-5700
WWW.ISSUESSHOP.COM

03-23-2019   13:34
REG   0010

DEPT02   T1 $16.95
DEPT02   T1 $8.99
DEPT02   T1 $8.50
DEPT02   T1 $6.99
DEPT02   T1 $5.00
DEPT02   T1 $3.00
TA1 $49.43
TAX1 $4.57
CHARGE $54.00
$54.00

all day—I was only there for a few hours. It just managed to pay its way, and no more.

Then there was another place opened in a basement in Rathbone Street called "The Dome"; and it was quite a nice place. It held about a hundred and fifty people, and it was a bit of a change because it was run by an Indian who was a friend of my friend who had the Bazaar in Brixton, and while it was being organized they asked me what I thought the scenery should be like. And I thought, "Well, they've seen places with Occult scenery and they've seen artists' murals, so for a change, it wouldn't be a bad idea to have some tropical scenery painted on the walls." So some poor artists got to work and they produced some very nice tropical scenery of palm trees and other colourful designs. In this establishment there was no bar. The sandwiches, snacks and the cups of tea and the coffee came up in a lift and through a trap-door, and they were collected on a tray by the waitress and taken round to the customers. This was their idea, which I thought was very good, doing away with the bar entirely. So I said to myself, "If ever I open a place again, there'll be no bar, just a trap-window."

I wasn't terrifically enthusiastic about opening another place. I was confronted with two problems: if I opened a School of Wisdom it would become too serious, and if I opened a place where I allowed variety and cabaret I would be invaded and I would have the same situation as I had at The Albatross, and I wouldn't be able to cope with the situation.

(This place in Rathbone Street, The Dome, it also got packed to suffocation.) So I decided not to bother for a bit.

And political activities quietened down a bit and life began to move a little bit more normally and various strange people floated into the West End. There was a good portion of our crowd used to go to the sea-side for the three months and fiddle the problem of existence by the sea-side, and come back in the winter. At this period I remember there was quite a big crowd of people at the Fitzroy Tavern, Charlotte Street, and quite a crowd at The Marquis of Granby, at the top of Rathbone Street. There was another character who was operating a cellar at Fitzroy Square. It was right off the beaten track because it was the top of Fitzroy Square. It was quite interesting because it was called "The Guy Fawkes". It had barrels for tables with wooden planks on top and a candlestick with candles in; and it had all kinds of chairs that cost about a shilling or two shillings apiece that were all painted different colours; and it had a big sheet of canvas which at some time had been the scenery in a theatre, and at each side of the canvas there were two terrific big trees—it was like an avenue looking out to the sea—and some artist had painted some ballet dancers dancing in the avenue and it looked very effective. This place was lit up with candles and you could get a cup of tea, but you couldn't get coffee. You could also get a bowl holding about two pints of soup and a chunk of bread for sixpence.

I told the proprietors, "You'll have to be very, very careful whom you let know about it, because it's certainly a fascinating den which our crowd, if they get to know about it, will like." And eventually my prediction was right. Some of our crowd, who liked to stop up till three or four o'clock in the morning, found this place and word went round. And they decided to have parties and there were parties going on there twice a week for about six weeks until some of the neighbours in Fitzroy Square started complaining about this Bohemian life going on until the early hours of the morning in a respectable vicinity; and the proprietor got the order to quit.

Then they had the same trouble at The Dome in Rathbone Street. They couldn't cope with the situation; they were packed to suffocation every night. I went there one night and it took all my time to get in. I did a turn there occasionally and there was somebody doing a tap-dance on a mat and there was a fire-eater and a girl who did the "Dance of the Seven Veils" (but she had tights on, so if the law had been there they couldn't have done anything); there was an accordion and two guitarists, and there was plenty of wine floating about the place brought in by some of the characters (in those days you could buy a good bottle of wine for two-and-six.)

I hadn't been operating for about two years. Now I was getting a change of environment; I was jumping about during the weekends with my Numerology board in the markets right out in the suburbs of London. One Saturday I'd go to Croydon Market; next Saturday I'd go to Walthamstow; the following Saturday I'd go to Shepherd's Bush, and the next Saturday I'd go to Acton Town Market. Sometimes I used to go to Brighton on the Workmen's train (the return fare was about three shillings) and the market there, in the centre of town, was also workable in those days, but it's not today. Another good market is Rathbone Street, Silvertown, the other side of Poplar; and Poplar itself was a good market on a Saturday. And all these markets were known to the people who had some method of fiddling an existence and they all used to leave the West End early Saturday mornings and go out to different markets.

Now there is a lot of characters whose names I have not mentioned, not because I'm frightened of them getting angry with me, but on principle. There are a lot of people to whom it would not be fair to divulge to the world their past activities. I can mention Prince Monolulu because everybody knows him. I've known him for several years and always have a chat or a cup of tea with him when I see him, and over the course of the years he's generally popped in and seen me when I've been running an establishment. He wrote his memoirs called *I've Got a Horse*.[32] A very, very likeable character and he has played his part in making events a bit decorative; he certainly brings a bit of sunshine into people's lives when they see him, because he's always dressed up in his regalia.

My rendezvous, which I used at this particular period, was a dive in Green's Court, off Berwick Street. It only held about twenty-five or thirty people and it consisted of four long tables, very much like dining-room tables, and there was a tiny bar in the corner where you got your tea and coffee and your snacks. Not many people knew of this place, only a very few of the outstanding characters, and this is where occasionally I used to like to hide myself. (Jinny was never a one for lounging about one of these places, she used to like her own studio.) In those days I always liked to stop out until about two or three o'clock in the morning and if I didn't work my astrology board in the afternoon I could always find somewhere to operate it at night.

In those days I could go and stand in a side street off Edgware Road and take a few shillings without being molested, but to-day I don't suppose you'd last more than about five minutes— you'd get packed up. The State has no intention of encouraging anybody to lead a Bohemian life. On top of that the key to the

32 *I Gotta Horse: the autobiography of Ras Prince Monolulu*. London: Hurst & Blackett, 1950.

great percentage of these people surviving by their abilities and their individualities was the Caledonian Market, and that's closed down now forever. Also everybody got confused and muddled-up with the war and those who didn't get muddled-up got their skates on. When they came back after the war they found that all the studios they used to have were all occupied as work-shops or tailors' shops or storerooms, and as a matter of fact, today there isn't anywhere where Bohemians can live in the West End. There are only about two cafés open all night—and this romantic, artistic life which I enjoyed, and many others enjoyed, is entirely gone with the wind. Also, at the very least, three-quarters of the characters are also gone with the wind. I do occasionally meet a few of them who are living in other towns and villages and have settled down for life and who have to discipline themselves to an orthodox, conventional life in order to get a living.

It was in this dive in Greens Court where I met a couple who had been in show business and they had been travelling around the Midlands with variety shows. The young lady was a dancer and her husband was a bit of an acrobat. They weren't new to the West End, they'd danced in several night clubs and she'd also seen me several times in my Bohemian Albatross Club. He had a little bit of money and I had a little bit (it was really handy to have a little bit in order to be able to do something which would carry you on your journey to the next situation which developed). So he said: "Have you got any ideas?" And I said, "Well, I think it would be possible to get an existence out of a rehearsal room, providing you could get us suitable premises. You could always let the room for an hour or two for a few shillings to anybody who wanted to do any rehearsing." And another brilliant idea I got was that my wife Jinny could organize a posing school: teaching girls how to pose. She'd done quite a lot of posing herself in side shows and *The World's Fair* (which is a paper that caters for show people) was always advertising for models for posing shows.

Anyway, this girl was quite good a dancer, she called herself "Lilies of the Valley." So I took her and her husband around to my studio and introduced them to Jinny and we had a discussion and we came to the conclusion that it wouldn't be a bad idea to try it out, and it might be a help in solving the problem of existence. So I got in touch with an estate agent. And in those days if you had a reputation of being able to pack a place to suffocation the agents were only too pleased to let you have premises because they knew that if you were operating it there wasn't a big chance of it being a financial failure. So I got a letter from an agent saying that he had premises on the roof in a building opposite Foyles in Charing Cross Road. We went up there and had a look at it and it had a pretty glass roof and I thought to myself, "Well, it's pretty large, it would hold at least two hundred people at once," but I thought to myself, "I won't use it as a society or meeting-place. I'll call it 'La Boheme' and make it an artists' rehearsal studio."

I soon got in touch with musicians who wanted to practise on their instruments and with amateur theatrical people who wanted to rehearse and I got in touch with some painters who would like to paint when the room was not used as a rehearsal room. I put a bar up so I could serve teas and coffees and mineral waters. And I operated La Boheme as a rehearsal room which, after all expenses were paid, brought us in a couple of pound a week each after we had paid somebody to run the catering side of it. I only used to go up there to sit for about an hour at night. I managed to get hold of some wicker chairs and some palm trees and some trestle-work and put up an artificial Spanish verandah with leaves growing all over it and subdued the lighting, and at night-time it was certainly a very nice atmosphere to lounge about in. The only thing I was sorry about was that it was on the top floor. If I could have had a building like that, with the same type of glass roof, on the ground floor with a piece of ground, I would have been happy for the rest of my life.

I made it a membership studio and I only allowed a certain section of the circle to know that it was operating, and it went on operating like that for nine months.

Then "Lilies of the Valley" got a booking for a tour in the North with her husband. It was the beginning of spring and I'd come right through the winter, and the two pounds a week I was getting out of the La Boheme assisted me in having a very comfortable existence, because I didn't have to do a lot of jumping about in order to get money to buy food with. I'd bought a piano, which was in very good condition, for six pounds and I had that put up there, and the people who used it for rehearsing told their friends about it and they came up and used it. But the thing which put me off it more than anything was that it was on the top floor.

So I then was introduced to an Indian (I had a lot of Indian friends) and he was looking for premises to run a club, so I sold him La Boheme for ten pounds. He moved in with his group and I moved out. There wasn't any scenery to take down because the landscapes were painted on the walls. And that was goodbye to La Boheme.

Now apart from the solving of the problem of existence, there was a Bohemian philosophy which most of the characters were aware of and which went far deeper than a lot of people realized. It wasn't a political philosophy, it was a philosophy which was more or less communal and could be applied to a group. Many characters were not satisfied with their orthodox and conventional learning, and it was an enthusiasm which penetrated into religions and philosophies that was not known about by the general public. Many characters were studying Buddhism, Zoroastrianism, the Druids, the Rosicrucians, and there were many little Occult groups who were not practising the Occult in the orthodox way, but were researching into it, trying to find out all they could about it. There were quite a lot of pamphlets floating about in this period of history and there were also a couple of weekly journals which put forward Bohemian ideas—I wrote a few articles in some of them.

The main basis of the Bohemian philosophy was that Creation came first, then the problem of existence, survival: to live and avoid all misery as much as possible—to live to live. They shared most of their lives with their colleagues. It was accepted that a man becomes what he does: it is Man who plans and creates; all that we are is the result of what we've done in the past. Reason alone must guide: the understanding of this philosophy destroys bondage and delusions—it's no good sitting and pining about the past—the strength of life is our own and we must live in ourselves, each according to his own acts and deeds. Harmony was the thing, and everybody strived for the development of the mind as it could be applied to life.

In this period of history Schopenhauer was very popular, and many of the thinkers in Hyde Park were advising the public to read *The Martyrdom of Man* by Winwood Reade, which could be bought in the Thinker's Library for a shilling.

The outstanding characters who were seen in and out of different places were Sylvia Goff,[33] Betty May,[34] and Nina Hamlet who wrote a book called *The Laughing Torso*.[35]

The markets were interesting in these days because there were one or two second-sight workers. These are people who went round a crowd and asked somebody for a commodity and then asked the lady that they had with them if she could describe what they had, which she could do quite easily. This was not easy to learn; it was worked by a very complicated code. It would entertain a crowd of people for about half an hour, and after the performance ended a lucky charm was sold, or a horoscope. There was a Punch and Judy show that used to come out at the weekends and work markets; there was also a ventriloquist who used to perform with his doll in the places I've mentioned. In the summer-time the West End occasionally was visited by Needies who were flogging perfumed bark, and they were dressed very picturesquely, like gipsies. Then there was another little group of people who called themselves the Dialectical Materialists; in discussions and in debates there were very few people who could hold their own with them. The background of some of these people was very interesting: a character called Cornelius, who was practising Astrology, was an actor.

The grafters—the characters who obtained their living by demonstrating commodities and fortune-telling, by Astrology or selling lucky charms—regularly went to the Derby, the Boat

---

33 This must be Sylvia Gough, the diamond heiress and former dancer, who had appeared in the Ziegfeld Follies.
34 Betty May (1893–c.1955) model, singer & dancer. Her book *Tiger Woman: my story* was published by Duckworth in 1929.
35 I think Jack means Nina Hamnett (1890–1956), the 'Queen of Bohemia', an artist and writer. Her book *Laughing Torso: Reminiscences of Nina Hamnett* was published by Constable & Co in 1932.

Race, Ascot, Henley Regatta and a variety of Fairs and Regattas all over the country. There is a paper (which I mentioned before) called *The World's Fair*, which is still in existence, and this paper gave the details of where all the fairs, carnivals and regattas were held. It also advertised for what it called grafters—that is, people who could talk to a crowd or work on a side-show or work in some show for a showman—and some characters were backwards and forwards through the season; they would have been travelling about with show people. It was a very important paper for those who fiddled to solve the problem of existence because it gave the address of all the warehouses in Great Britain where novelties and cheap jewellery could be bought. It also had one page which was called "The Grafters' Corner," and on this page there would be related the lives of different grafters, what part of the country they were travelling in, if they changed from one game to another, their abilities of talking to a crowd, and also giving interesting articles on grafters of the past—and sometimes about me, Ironfoot Jack. I also used to go to Henley Regatta myself, and Ascot and the Derby, and at this period I was tipping by Numerology. The race-course in these days was very interesting because there was quite a lot of professional tipsters, and also all kinds of grafters and performers were allowed to perform on the free courses.

Now one of the most amazing things, which proves that there was a terrific brotherhood of sincerity amongst these people who lived a precarious life, was that when they were floating in and out of the West End and they met you, they would ask, "Where do they all go now?" Well, in this period of history there was no set big place for them to go to. Most of the places had gone with the wind, but a variety of little tiny places opened, and it was quite simple in those days to open a place on ten pounds. Once you got in possession of a basement, or ground floor flat, the Caledonian Market was the solution, because up there you could buy chairs at a shilling or two shillings apiece, and you could buy timber to make tables with and you could paint all these tables and these chairs different colours, and if you were one of the circle, there were always plenty of poor artists who would come along and paint murals on the wall, and there were musicians who liked to practise on their guitars and who'd come along and entertain the company at night.

In the side streets round about Charlotte Street and Berwick Street, and in other little streets in Soho, there were quite a lot of little bookshops who obtained their living by selling second-hand books. Most of these books were bought amongst the junk in the Caledonian Market and also along Farringdon Road, and there were quite a few people who obtained a living by fiddling about selling books.

There was plenty of orthodox and conventional cafés, some of them all-night, but these cafés were not used by the Bohemians. And there were basements in Charlotte Street and Bloomsbury where you could go down and have a cup of tea or coffee and they were meeting places only for our crowd. There was one called "The Pentagram," and another called "The Blue Star" in Charlotte Street both of which held about thirty people.

There was a Dr. Johnson, a very charming and lovable character, who knew an enormous amount of the Bohemians in Soho and the West End, and he was considered the greatest authority on Hegelian philosophy. Cosmo was about in those days; he was a hypnotist and occasionally he frequented some of these cafés and gave demonstrations of his hypnotic abilities. And there were poets who wrote their own pamphlets and walked around flogging them, and there were parties somewhere every weekend.

There was another little place, a ground-floor place, in Hanway Street, off Tottenham Court Road, which was known as "The Hanway" and it was used for some period, mostly by buskers, grafters and Hyde Park orators, but occasionally some of the other characters used to float in and out. After The Dome closed in Rathbone Place, it re-opened again and its proprietors were Indians and it was called "The Last Chance" and it was just a tea and coffee lounge; on the wall there was two beautiful silk tapestries, one of the Taj Mahal and one of the Lucky Elephant called Ganesh—this place became a meeting-place for the characters who were interested in Yoga philosophy.

The poor artists used to come round and flog their paintings in and out of these places, and the Countess Minicci (she was a very well-known Italian character) floated in and out of these places. At this period she was doing flower paintings with her fingers. She was a very likeable character, very generous, and when she sold three or four pictures she generally threw a party at her studio for her friends.

There was a variety of very unusual pamphlets being flogged and there was this pamphlet by a character who'd had something to do with the law and got the nickname of "I Haven't Got Any Money." This is a copy of the pamphlet which he was flogging for tuppence. I am glad that I've found a copy amongst my collection of documents because it is rather humorous, and it gives some idea of how conditions were developing at this particular period of the history of the West End:

"*My Dear Sir,*

Regarding your request for money, for the following reasons I unable to send you the sum suggested.

I have been held up, held down, sand-bagged, I have been walked upon, squeezed and flattened out, by Income Tax, the Sugar Tax, the Motor Tax, the Spirit Tax, Beer Tax and Tobacco Tax, to say nothing of the Entertainment Tax, Super-Tax and by every Body, Society and Group that the inventive mind of man can think of to extract that which I may or may not have in my possession, for the Red Cross, the Black Cross and the Double Cross, and for every Charity and Institution existing in the country.

The Government has governed my business until I do not know who runs it, they or I. I have been inspected, examined, re-examined, informed, required and commanded until I do not know where I am, who I am, and if I am on my head or my feet.

All I know is that I am supposed to be an inexhaustible supply of money for every need, desire or hope of the human race and because I will not go out and beg, borrow or steal money to give away I am cussed, discussed, boycotted, talked to, talked about, held up, hung up, rung up and robbed. The only reason I cling to life at all is just to see how long one can stick it out and to see what can possibly happen next.

Yours Faithfully."

He was a very lovable character. He camped out in a sleeping-bag nearly all the year round, and he was always advising people to read *Candide*, by Voltaire.

There was a Freedom Club that had a basement in Charlotte Street and they were mostly discussing the philosophy of Mikhail Bakunin, Proudhon, and *The Cry For Justice* by Upton Sinclair,[36] and they were advocating a better system of society. Then there were other circles who were attempting to stimulate themselves by creating new theories of religion which were not appertaining to the worship of the Supernatural, but were appertaining to the worship of the Cosmos. I had a friend who was one of the leading lights of the Druids, and he was seen in several of these places and they used to float from one place to the other.

Very occasionally my wife Jinny came to some of these places and I used to collect her at night when I had come from a market or I'd been to another town. Although she didn't join any political party she was very militant and stimulated herself going to societies which were advocating the emancipation of women. She also used to be fond of reading the memoirs of women who had led a precarious life, and one of the books she used to recommend her lady-friends to read was *The Memoirs of Susan Lennox*,[37] and the book she liked more than any was *The Memoirs of Isadora Duncan*[38]—in many ways, she had the same type of temperament as Isadora Duncan. On many occasions she asked me my views on the subject and I always told her that, so far as women were concerned, if they didn't like the system they lived under—the system I wanted no part of—it was up to them to do something about it.

36 *The Cry for Justice: An Anthology of the Literature of Social Protest.* NY & Pasadena CA: Privately Published, 1915.
37 I think that Jack may be referring to a novel by David Graham Phillips (1867–1911) entitled *Susan Lenox: her fall and rise.* Published in parts by *Hearst's Magazine* in 1913 and filmed in 1931 with Greta Garbo.
38 Actually entitled *My Life.* London: Victor Gollancz, 1928.

We also had one or two good women speakers, and if guitars and mandolins were not playing in the different rendezvous studios there was always a discussion going on somewhere about something interesting.

Most of the grafters—that is, the people who obtained their living on markets—had started a grafter's life at twenty or twenty-five and they'd remained, most of them, at this particular type of existence all their lives. There were some isolated cases where one or two launched into a little fiddling business, into a shop, and sold commodities, and some of them managed to accumulate money to start themselves up in clutter shops and second-hand bookshops and bric-a-brac, Victorian jewellery, and knick-knacks and odds and ends. None of them really could get beyond the position of a comfortable existence because there were hundreds of these clutter and fiddling shops all over the place.

With a little bit of money in those days it was quite possible to get unfurnished places, and for a few pounds in the Caledonian Market you could furnish a nice little home with odds and ends of carpets and furniture. Most of the poor Bohemians were not interested in furniture; so long as they obtained an unfurnished basement or cellar they were satisfied with a divan and blankets, and the rest of the furniture was knocked out of timber and orange boxes and tea-cases. And the cellars were either decorated with murals or velvet or cretonne curtains. There were several artists who got a living making weird and fantastic masks out of plaster of Paris also copying Chinese and Indian masks painted in a variety of very outstanding bright colours, and these masks were flogged in and out of these certain places for three or four bob. As I've mentioned before, three or four bob and you'd solved the problem of existence for the day.

There were a lot of characters who were always able to smoke because they would buy half an ounce of cigarette tobacco, mix it with an ounce of herbal tobacco, and roll their own cigarettes.

If any of the characters got into hospital from misfortune there was always plenty of people to go up and see them, and take them fruit and books—all the characters that I've mentioned were known by a great percentage of the characters that were floating around those days; everybody knew everybody else.

A little farther up Goodge Street there was another cellar which was called "Daisy's Dive." Daisy had been in Variety and was a tap-dancer; she had her own clientele, her friends were in and out of small repertory companies and also did a bit of crowd work in films.

There was also another small crowd who were constantly going from the West End to Paris and were more or less organized in a small way in Montparnasse, so we used to get the news of what was going on in Paris amongst the Bohemians.

For at least three years there was no big establishment operating in the West End for Bohemians. I was dreaming about opening a big establishment that would hold about three hundred people—I was dreaming about it, and I turned it over several times in my mind but I wasn't terrifically enthusiastic about it because I'd already had an experience of what I would have to put up with. I knew that what might happen was that it would get so well-known that it would be invaded by all kinds of sight-seers, and unless I had very powerful help to co-operate with me I'd have too much on my plate. However, I just carried on and dreamed about the place and how I would decorate it…

Now some of those that fell into this type of life were characters who had been leading an orthodox, conventional life and had saved a little bit of money, and either they had matrimonial trouble or else they became frustrated with the monotony of routine—the same thing, over and over again. They generally arrived with a little bit of money, say thirty or forty pounds, and they would mingle with our crowd and it would take them a few weeks before they fitted in. When they had been seen around for about a month or so they were more-or-less accepted as part and parcel of this set-up. There was a fluctuation in and out all the time, and occasionally some of these characters would inherit wealth or they would inherit property. They didn't become orthodox mentally, but they became orthodox physically by going back to an orthodox, conventional life. I met several characters who were running small successful businesses in different towns and they said, "Well, I remember you from when I used to live in the West End. And I don't regret my experience as I learned more about life through this particular experience than I could learn anywhere else."

There were very few books that told anything about this subject, and the only book in existence at that period which gave a short explanation of how people got their living on fair grounds was a book called *Cheap-Jack*, and the name of the author could only be obtained by enquiring at *The World's Fair* offices in Oldham. This book explained different kinds of fiddling on fair grounds, but it had no information at all about how people fiddled to survive between the West End and the Caledonian Market.[39]

There were successful antique dealers that used to mingle with this crowd, also successful book dealers, occasionally

---

39 I think this might be *The Life and Adventures of a Cheap Jack: by one of the fraternity* edited by Charles Hindley (William Green). London: Tinsley Brothers, 1876.

orthodox doctors, and there were some very successful business-men who used to like to talk to these people and used to assist them financially in a small way. The Press had its reporters floating around trying to collect interesting material, but they really didn't know the depth of it and they didn't know what it was all about.

There was a character who'd never been to an art school who we called "Dreamy," and he had a cellar in Allan Street. I went to his den to have a cup of tea one day, and he had a collection of Mexican drawings of weird and fantastic imaginary elemental gods. Three had been done by quite a good artist and these he would trace and reproduce in water-colours; he always produced them on old seventeenth century sheets of paper—he could always buy an old book for thruppence or fourpence and tear the blank, plain leaves out of it—and he had his own method of dirtying his inks and his water-colours. He used to produce two or three of these Mexican drawings and put them in old frames which you could buy in clutter shops for tuppence or thruppence apiece, and he used to walk around flogging these. They were quite fascinating, very similar to the gods and idols worshipped by the Maoris of New Zealand. (In his younger days he'd been a merchant seaman.) His cellar walls were plastered with picture frames from these fascinating drawings and he could quite easily flog three a day, at three shillings apiece. The only books that he had in his studio were books appertaining to primitive art. He had a divan and a blanket and one or two bits of furniture which he had made out of orange boxes, and he coated these orange boxes with one colour of paint, and then traced some primitive design and painted it in fantastic colours. His philosophy was that of a Pagan. And his favourite book was Marcus Aurelius' *Meditations*. (All these characters had their favourite book which they more or less considered as their Bible.) He also had no trouble in flogging his primitive water-colours in the Caledonian Market, and in various clutter shops. He had no competition in this racket. He was always very generous, and although he led the life, more or less, of a lone wolf, he found his companionship with various characters.

There was also a character called "Old Bill". He had a walrus moustache and had served in the First World War. He used to play a mandolin in doorways in the early hours of the morning around Oxford Street and Piccadilly. And another called "Matinavi" who used to recite Shakespeare to the theatre queues.

Then there was this cartoon artist who used to do quick sketch cartoons. He used to go round and collect a pile of newspaper placards and he'd fasten these placards on an easel, and set this down in front of the theatre queue and he'd do cartoons of famous politicians and film stars of that day and obtain his living by collecting from the queue. He was writing a book about characters who were to be found round coffee stalls! But it was only a small pamphlet in a paper cover, and on the front page of the book he'd drawn a cartoon of a tramp. The book started off in a very flowery and fantastic style:

There's a life in London while all its citizens are asleep. It's not the life of the night clubs or the drinking dens, but it's the drama of human life where people who are deprived of their night's sleep are drawn to the lights of coffee stalls like moths round a candle. In this drama old faces go and new faces come, and yet the drama goes on and on.

And he described, according to his theory, how these various characters got there. His favourite book was also *The Cry for Justice* by Upton Sinclair. He didn't belong to any particular party, but in the summer-time, after he'd solved the problem of existence he'd argue the point in Hyde Park until twelve o'clock at night, and then he'd come into one of the Bohemian dives and he'd find somebody to have an argument with. He loved to argue— this stimulated him. He lived in a cellar at the back of The Seven Dials with another character who used to go round pubs playing a banjo, made-up like "Chirgwin, the One-Eyed Kaffir."[40]

There was a woman about forty-five who used to stand in café doorways, and she used to hold a small hurdy-gurdy in her hand and she used to sing, not too loudly, "She Was a Dear Little Dicky-Bird" and "Daisy, Daisy, a Bicycle Built for Two." She had rather a cultured and a refined voice and was very polite but nobody knew anything of her background.

And there was also another woman who was very cultured and refined, and she used to come out about eleven o'clock at night until one o'clock in the morning. She was a very good singer and would draw quite a good crowd, but she did not sing to any music. She was very attractive and wore a long, wide, black skirt and a pullover, with a Spanish comb at the back of her long hair and a Spanish shawl which had embroidered coloured flowers on it. And she was known to some people as "Lena". Nobody could find out anything about her background either, or where her studio dive was, and yet many of these characters I am describing now were around for some years.

40 I think Jack must mean 'Chirgwin the *White-Eyed* Kaffir'. George Chirgwin (1854–1922) was a British music hall performer who employed a blacked-up face which he adapted by leaving a white diamond shape over one eye.

There was another character who used to play a terrific big trumpet (about the biggest trumpet you could possibly obtain) and he got the name amongst our crowd of "Go Away." He used to kick up such a terrific row on this shocking trumpet that people used to throw pennies at him to go away and also in the afternoon he would annoy people in offices round Wardour Street. He would get in the doorway of a pub or café, and would generally get a penny for him to go away. Well, that didn't worry him. If he got a penny everywhere he went he could easily collect three or four shillings and so solve the problem of existence that way. But he wasn't welcomed in any of our places after he'd finished annoying people; he was generally found in the early hours of the morning around the coffee stalls in Covent Garden Market.

There were a few characters who, when they were really hard up, went round Covent Garden Market to collect what vegetables they could find. If you found vegetables in the gutter in those days they were yours; you could also take a trip down at three or four o'clock in the morning to the Fish Market in Billingsgate where you could buy for fourpence enough cods' heads to keep you for two days. As a matter of fact, when a cod's head is boiled it makes quite a good meal. All these little secrets it was necessary to know. And of course going into different butcher's shops and buying little bits of odd meat that were lying all over the counter, known as "block ornaments," for fourpence you'd get enough meat, if you added three penn'orth of vegetables to it, to make a stew to keep four people—as much as they could eat—for two days. In those days there was food in abundance for a few coppers if you knew how to get the few coppers, and how to manipulate them. You could get a box of stale cakes for tuppence, enough to keep you for two days; you could get a box of broken biscuits for tuppence; you could get a box of "specked" and squashed fruit in any greengrocers late at night for thruppence. And if you went to a grocer's shop and asked for tuppence worth of cheese cuttings, you'd get about two pounds of cheese in bits and pieces. One meal which was often served up in buskers' studios would be cheese cuttings (which had the cloth rind cut off) chopped up in a saucepan with half a pint of milk, and a pound of boiled onions. You poured this over two thick slices of bread on a plate. All this didn't come to more than a shilling, including a penny in the gas to cook it. And this was quite a good banquet for two people, if you were hungry. And nearly everybody in those days was sprinkling curry on their food no matter what the meal was!

But there was nobody who predicted that one day this delightful type of life which these people were leading, including myself, would be shattered. Nobody predicted that eventually there would be a war, and after the war the Caledonian Market would be shut forever. Nobody predicted that when all those characters, who'd got involved in the war in some way or the other, came back there would be no cellars or basements which they could occupy for a cheap rent and turn into studios and so go back to the enjoyable life which they were leading before the war. When they came back they found the hundreds of basements and cellars which once were occupied by people who considered themselves "Bohemians" now being used as workshops and storerooms and little manufacturing businesses. To many this was a great tragedy. What happened to a lot of the characters? Some have presumably gone with the wind; some of them have evaporated into the elements, and quite a lot have settled in villages, small towns and industrial cities all over the England.

Occasionally I meet some of them that I haven't seen for years who come up to the West End to have a look round at weekends, and a great percentage of them are now forced to lead an orthodox and conventional life to survive. There are almost no cafés open all night; where there were fifty or sixty open all night in the West End, there are now only about three. There's a few night clubs open until about three or four o'clock in the morning, but most of them are "clip" joints.

There's no doubt that this artistic and romantic life that we led is now entirely gone with the wind, never to return—impossible to return—because this was like a colony: we had somewhere to live right in the heart of the West End and we also had the Caledonian Market, which was the mainstay of solving the problem of existence in those days.

Even the jumping about from town to town and getting a living by fiddling or selling a commodity is a thing of the past today, because I don't know of any towns that have got what they call a "nethers kenners"—a place where travellers put up for the night—and if you went to a strange town for the night now they'd want at least ten shillings Bed and Breakfast, and on top of that it would be an impossibility to scrounge any food out of the shops. If you went round the shops in London and in the country or even in an industrial town, you'd have a job! If it was summertime you could get somewhere to camp for your sleeping-bag, but you don't get any cheap food anymore. The only way you might survive is by "rag-a-boning." There'd be very few towns and villages where you would be able to do any busking, you might, in some towns, be able to do a theatre queue—but what I can see of it, it's finished. In the old days any stranger could go to any market town and get a livelihood; now all the markets, all over Great Britain, are monopolized by the local people and they certainly don't encourage characters who are orators and get a crowd round them. And you wouldn't solve the problem of existence with Astrology because so many newspapers and journals have got paragraphs in them: "What the Stars Have in Store for You;" "The Signs of the Zodiac;" "What the Stars Foretell" etc...so the competition in that particular angle has been so terrific that you just couldn't survive.

Occasionally I get a charabanc[41] from Victoria to Southampton or the train up to Great Yarmouth and hitch-hike from village to village and town to town back to London, but I have not seen any Needies on the road and I've not seen any professional tramps. I've seen a few gipsies and most of these are settled on their own ground—that is to say, a town or village—and they get their living flogging or totting and they travel nowhere near as much as they did in my days, when I was on the road. I should say the Needies are practically extinct in Great Britain—they couldn't survive!

There's a few of the old-time buskers left in the West End, just a few. There's the "Lunar Boys," they've been tap-dancing round the West End for about twenty years; they do comical tap-dancing and taking off various characters; and there's another crowd who call themselves "The Happy Wanderers;" they're comical tap-dancers, they dance to an accordion. But all the other buskers that I knew, and also the pavement artists and the characters who produced weird commodities and fiddled them, they're all gone with the wind. Roger Cane, who was the greatest cartoon artist in the West End, died just after the war, and Old Bill, the mandolin-player, he died just after the war...and

41 "Carriage with benches": old-fashioned name for a bus.

many of those characters even the old-timers don't know what's happened to them, or what's become of them. There's another very nice character known as "Skeeter" who has obtained his living for years racing and also doing cartoons for jockeys in pubs in the local towns where the races took place. I've seen him several times but he's not known to the rising generation—the only places that they have to meet are the coffee houses. But out of the thousands of people who fiddled an existence, today I don't suppose I could mention more than about ten. Even those now have to rely on their pensions. It's a drama that is all over, and becoming history to the sociologists.

There are very few markets left, even around London, where you can buy second-hand books. I've been in dozens of markets round about London lately and I haven't seen any book stalls at all. I've seen just one or two clutter stalls with bric-a-brac and Victorian jewellery and I often wonder how they get a living at it because I've had a go at it myself and I can't get a living with a clutter stall. In the first place you've got to buy your clutter, and you've got to pay ten times as much for it as you did before the war; in the second place you've got to pay ten shillings (or a pound if it's a private market) for a pitch for the day; on top of that you've got to pay three or four shillings for the rent of the stall; and even if you go down the Walworth Road, the temporary licence is three-and-six. So there's four shillings for the rent of the stall, and then there's the amount of money you have to lay out for your clutter (clutter means second-hand books, little bits of china, beads, fans, little boxes and snuff-boxes, ornaments, Victorian jewellery, second-hand cutlery, little decorative pictures—the word 'clutter' covers those commodities, if they are second-hand); and after you've paid your stall and paid your temporary licence and your fare to get there, if you'd earn five shillings after standing all day you'd be very lucky.

In these days I wouldn't be at all surprised if markets eventually didn't nearly become extinct, because the markets of those days were more interesting. The public used to look forward to going down there and listening to the peculiar characters talking about different subjects and the quack doctors that were about in that day certainly did a lot of studying and were interesting to listen to. It was their oratory that helped to sell the commodity. You could stand there all day and, if you didn't say a word about the commodities, you'd be lucky if you took three shillings.

The thing which has probably put the Needies out of action more than anything is Woolworths, because a lot of Needie women had a hawker's licence, and they used to go hawking brushes and combs and needles and threads and an enormous variety of knick-knacks which you can now buy in Woolworths.[42] I have also been told that it's very difficult to get a hawker's licence today. So as far as the Needies are concerned we say "Good-bye" to those romantic characters of the road.

Now all these characters, who comprised a variety of people wanting to know each other and also interested in each other's well-being, were definitely an existing order of what I would call "mental socialism"—that is to say were all more or less concerned about how each other was getting on. They enquired about one another, they went to the funeral of any of the characters when they evaporated into the elements or to the wedding when they married.

---

42 In the early days of trading, most items in F. W. Woolworth stores were priced at either 3d or 6d; a serious threat to market traders.

A character or a scholar becomes an outstanding and a very interesting person when he acquaints himself with any curious learning. Unfortunately the books dealing with curious learning are very difficult to find. There are various Occult Circles who possess them but unless you are proposed and seconded to become a member of these circles it's impossible for you to get any knowledge about this curious learning. I've always, for my enjoyment, been interested in this curious learning more than anything else. It was the School of Wisdom where the Vice president, Mr. Munn, and the Secretary, Carl Crane, introduced me to all the varieties of Schools which I had great enjoyment in studying. There's the Meditation Sect, the Pure Light Sect, the Exotic Sect, the Mahayana Sect and when I came to discover Cosmic Dynamics, I got all the philosophy here which, as far as I was concerned, became more than a belief.

Now I have no intention of boring anybody with highbrow gymnastics, and I have no intention of advising or persuading anybody to believe in the conclusions that I've come to. It's a very good thing to wade into different beliefs because eventually, providing you do enough wading, you get hold of some kind of philosophy which stimulates you and is also an asset when applied to the activities of life.

GIPSY ORIGINS AND CHARACTERS:
FAIRGROUND LIFE

Now I'll describe to you a little bit about gipsies and also a little bit about their languages, and the "Jogars Polary" which is the language of the buskers—that is, the travelling musicians—also the language which is used by the Needies when they want to talk between themselves.

During my research into literature to try and find out as near as possible the origin of gipsies, that in bygone days were called "vagabonds," it has been a complicated problem trying to find authentic material about them. Sir W. Jones' *Asiatic Researches*, Volume 3, page vii,[43] suggests that they might, in some particular expedition, have landed on the coast of Arabia or Africa. They were much versed in Astronomy, which in early days was little else than Astrology. There is scarcely any country in Europe that hasn't had gipsies and they have gone under different names: in France they were called "Bohemians" and in some other countries they were called "Tartars." They were supposed to have made their first appearance in Germany in 1517, and travelled with a train of hunting-dogs, like the nobles. Pope Pius II, who died in 1464, mentions them under the name of

43 A series of transactions published in the late eighteenth century under the auspices of Sir William Jones (1746–1794).

"Zitari" who were supposed to have migrated from "Cigi" which nearly answers to "Circassia." Another authority asserts that they came from Hindustan and part of their language is supposed to be Hindustani; other authorities suppose them to be a class of Indians, or "Pariahs Sudras." The estimate of these wanderers all over Europe goes into thousands (this is another controversy) and in 1560 they were banished. Under this order they dispersed into little companies and spread themselves all over Europe. Some of them were supposed to have arrived from Spain in 1591 and the first time they appeared, according to accounts, in England was in the reign of Henry VIII, in the year 1530.

Part of this material I copied from an old manuscript dated 1834 which I found in a clutter shop in Southampton.

According to another document, which I consider as authentic, they had the secrets of the reading of the Tarot Cards. They did not write down the formulas of how to read the cards but they handed down the knowledge to one another verbally, from generation to generation. In another history of Alchemy and Magicians there is a magician who was supposed to have abstracted the formula of how to read Tarot Cards, and to-day there is a variety of small books giving details about how to read them. These cards are very serious because they portray the drama of Life in Human Existence. I knew a clairvoyant who used to give readings with the Tarot Cards; she had a studio in Bayswater and she used to charge as much as a guinea for a reading. (Although she wasn't a gipsy she had led, in her early days, a gipsy life, and she'd revisited them and could talk a little bit of Romany.) A proper reading of the Tarot Cards, would take at least an hour. This lady called herself "Madame Polary" and "polary" means "to talk." She occasionally used to come into one or two of the dives in the West End and I used to talk a little bit of Romany to her. She couldn't talk Romany fluently, nor could I, because at the early period of my life there wasn't any available literature describing the Romany language.

Now providing you can talk a little Romany you are always welcome amongst gipsies, not permanently, but you are welcome for a short time if you can say a few words like "cushty" or "boner" or some of the words I will now give you: "ta rakka"—to talk; "vi vado"—the caravan; "vi gry"—the horse; "poo the gry"—put the horse out to grass; "omee"—man; "scarpering omee"—policeman; "dooker"—be able to read the hand, do Palmistry; "bewer"—woman; "baree manisha"—beautiful woman; "pikies"—children; "kenner"—house; "monkery"—place where they are living; "tober"—fairground.

In the old days the real historical gipsies who were telling fortunes had beautifully constructed gipsy caravans that could cost anything from a hundred to a thousand pounds; these were the wealthy class of the gipsies, and this class was mostly descended from the genuine historical gipsies. There was a poorer class of gipsies—they had coconut shies on fair grounds, and another class of gipsies that were on the road in my days and made their living dealing in ponies and horses at fairs and with farmers. There was another class who were in contact with a warehouse somewhere in England which imported reproduction carpets, Oriental bedspreads and a variety of wall tapestries and they travelled about the country-side flogging carpets, mats and bedspreads. They were more wealthy and they were also descended from the genuine historical gipsies and travelled in very expensive caravans which were ordered and made by firms on the Continent and in England who specialised in making that type of caravan. But there is a theory that the original gipsy caravan is the one that they make themselves which has a canvas bow (or circular) top, and for years there have been all kinds of controversies about how and from where these people originated.

The gipsies were sympathetic to the Needies but you will very seldom find them living together. Needies may be living the gipsy life but they are not descendants of the early gipsies who came to Britain as mentioned earlier. I have a theory that possibly during some period of history when families were evacuating their farms and other people from cities were going out into the country, squatting on land, and claiming it as their own, some of these city dwellers or farmers got hold of various types of farmyard carts with four wheels and made themselves home-made caravans and called themselves "Needies".

Those Needies that I was brought up with, travelled in families with tents and ponies and traps, and I've already described how they got a living. I might mention here that I am Australian by birth; I was born in Sydney. And from then, 1882, to now, 1956, is a great gap and I can't remember anything about Australia. All I can remember is being brought to England, being put into a boarding school, running away from school and, a few months later, jogging along the lanes of Kent with the Needies. So from that time onwards I've always considered myself to be one of them—a Needie gipsy which I became through learning the secrets and the strange language of Romany, which is now almost lost in antiquity…

Anyway, all these people were a great brotherhood of wanderers. I never regret what I learned from them; I could never have learned from any professor at any university all I learned from these people—and you can absorb in your mind an encyclopaedia of knowledge but this will not assist you in solving the problem of existence. To be able to solve this problem without settling into an orthodox and conventional routine you have to know some knowledge that is kept very secret. Some of this knowledge I am giving to you in *The Surrender of Silence*—my Memoirs.

Now the true gipsies and the Needies looked upon the whole of conventional society as "flatties". They're not antagonistic to them but they're entirely apart. As far as they are concerned literature, art and philosophy are meaningless. The only thing they appreciate is music and in those days their main entertainment was guitars, tambourines and mouth-organs. The Needies brought up their children to solve the problem of existence by making use of the same crafts that they were taught: "totting," "china-faking," "mush-faking," selling perfumed bark and lucky charms, hawking around the doors with various knick-knacks etc.

The Needies used one or two gipsy words, and some words that originally were used by the buskers, so I'm not going to say that all the words that follow are strictly Jogars Polary—that is: the wandering minstrels' language used by the Needies—but I will give you some of the words I know: "polary"—talk; "farmee" or "groinee"—ring; "daisies"—a pair of boots; "miltog"—shirt; "smother"—overcoat; "whistle"—suit; "capeller"—hat; "thomix" or "mazuma"—money; "gorge"—man; "tray"—thruppence; "soldee"—sixpence; "dinar"—shilling; "parunbeeonk"—half a crown. Some of this language has floated into the market places and became market slang: "caser" or "dollar"—five shillings; "nicker"—one pound; "ton"—a hundred pounds; "half-ton"—fifty pounds.

Some of these words have floated into racing slang and into the slang of the underworld: "peter"—a suitcase, is used by the underworld as slang for a prison cell or a safe. "Mincers on your bins"—keep your eyes open, is used in racing slang.

To do a "skipper" is to sleep under a hedge, or in a barn, but to sleep outside with nothing to keep you warm is doing a "starry." This was used by someone who was completely "on the floor" and "skint to the wide" which means they haven't got a penny to bless themselves with and have got no idea of how to fiddle a few coppers. Forty years ago there were a lot of these people who were down and out and didn't know how to fiddle. They used to make a bee-line for the seaside towns and smoke butt-ends and find what they could to eat in the dustbins that were hanging from lamp-posts on the promenade or in the railway station. Now, thank goodness, we have the Welfare State and their misery is over.

To "jogar" is to play a musical instrument. This is a Needie and a busker word, and to "jogar and drag" is to walk up and down the street playing your instrument. To "grizzle" is to sing, and an "ankeeohme" is a person who can do a "slang"—that is: either performing with chains or a strait-jacket, or doing an acrobatic feat, or dancing to an accordion, or bending bars of iron. There were a few Needies who obtained their living by performing in market places bending nails and bars of iron and tearing books in half with their hands, but you don't see them about today. This is what is known as "slanging to a pitch"—performing to a crowd of people. In those days—I'm talking about forty years ago now—four market workers might club together and they would buy a cart to travel about with (in those days you could buy a good second-hand cart for five pounds), and in the summer-time they would travel about from "gaff to gaff." A "gaff" is a place where there is either a regatta, a fair or a carnival.

Occasionally you'll find a gipsy who is a scholar, and by that I mean a person who has waded deeply into Literature, Music, Art and Philosophy. And occasionally you will find a Needie who is a scholar; there's quite a lot of buskers who were scholars and there's quite a lot of market workers who were scholars too; there were even occasionally stall-holders who were scholars.

Now there was a very interesting character, we called him Ben; he could speak several languages very fluently; he was also a merchant seaman. In his younger days he'd been a hobo in America and he'd bummed his way round Canada (that is to say, he led a life of a hobo). He arrived in the West End about twenty years ago, and he's still around—of course he's an old man now—and every time I meet him I have a cup of tea and a nice chat. During the course of the twenty years he signed on merchant ships which went from here to the Continent, but when he got to the Continent he generally used to make it his business to go adrift there and bum around. He would only take part-time jobs to survive; he'd worked on building sites and he'd done pearl-diving (by which is meant washing dishes) and fruit-picking on farms. He used to like to work for about six months and then to bum around for six months. His main method of getting a living when he was bumming around was by going to a tourist office where they required linguists to accompany people touring around the Continent. His knowledge of towns and cities in Germany, Switzerland, France, Italy and Belgium was colossal, and if he happened to be in London in the summer-time he used to seek out Norwegians and chat to them in their own language (which he spoke fluently). Ben was definitely a descendant of the Needies and a very, very likeable character. He carried on a lifetime like this and accumulated enough money to make himself a caravan which he put on his sister's land and camped out with her (she also had a caravan and made her living by hawking). He never married but had several love affairs.

There were a few people I traced who were descendants of Needie gipsies. I should think that, during the course of my experience in the West End, I met at least thirty or forty of them. Some of them had their caravans down at Lea Bridge, and they used to come into the West End at night-time selling cheap reproduction prayer mats that probably were imported from Morocco or Algeria. The Bohemians liked these mats because they were very colourful and looked nice when hung on a wall.

While all this was going on, the "underworld" kept to itself on the other side of Shaftesbury Avenue, the cafés round Shaftesbury Avenue and Wardour Street and Lisle Street and Rainbow Corner, and in and out the back streets of Frith Street and other little side streets of Soho. This is where the so-called "underworld" was supposed to be found. In those days the Bohemians kept themselves well within the vicinity of Charlotte Street, and the dives that were operated at this period of history were more or less Bohemian lounges and were run by one of the characters and they were kept very exclusively to one circle. There was, round Charlotte Street, one ground-floor basement called "The Lantern." And there were artists who had studios from one end of Charlotte Street to the other, in the garrets, and they used to spend their time painting all day and some of them used to go out and get orders for commercial designs and commercial painting.

Another great friend of mine was a dealer who lived in Howland Street. His name was Bill, and sometimes Bill would be in my company for a week; he was a great friend of my wife Jinny, and my wife was with me altogether twenty-five years before she evaporated into the elements...However, why I was so attached to Bill was because his parents were also the descendants of Needies. They had a scrapyard somewhere in Brixton and they dealt in rags and metal. Bill used to buy his commodities in salerooms; he used to get all the catalogues, and look up all the sales, and he would go to a sale about twice or three times a week. He knew quite a lot about expensive antiques but he kept mostly to brass trays and brass figures, and Chinese vases and Satsuma vases and Cloisonne vases and Blue Canton and, on many occasions, I used to flog a lot of his stuff for him. Now he was known in the trade as a "runner" and when I was getting my living by this particular method, I was also known as a "runner". This means that I had to know a little bit about antiques: jade and ivory, Worcester, Crown Derby, Chelsea etc. Runners would not bother about furniture, they kept to the commodities which they could carry in an attaché case or a kitbag. They would buy in one clutter shop to sell to another and they bought in salerooms and sold direct to the trade.

Bill was always in touch with me and round this period of his life he married a girl who was a daughter of a hawker—they were settled down in Brixton with a little shop and a house and they became wardrobe dealers.[44] And, when the war was on, Bill was in First Aid, and he had some very nasty experiences in the London air raids and eventually he came and lived with me and Jinny in my cottage at Oxford—which I will describe later in this story.

44 By "wardrobe dealers" Jack means sellers of second-hand clothing.

Then there was another profession which was only known to a few people. It was known as "slapping" (the secret word for it among dealers). For some time during the war, jumping round about Oxford, I had a go at this particular type of profession to get a living. You had a pamphlet published with your name on it, and it said:

Dear Sir or Madam,

This is my introduction. I beg to inform you that I shall have the pleasure of calling on you shortly.

I am paying the highest prices for discarded antiques, whatever the condition may be. Any of the following items for disposal: BRASS, COPPER, SILVER, BRONZE, IVORY, JADE and CRYSTAL, SNUFF-BOXES, CAMEOS, CANDLESTICKS, MINIATURES, PLAQUES, MEDALLIONS, FIGURES, COLOURED PRINTS, or any discarded JEWELLERY, OLD BOOKS and any junk at all of this description.

Turn your ANTIQUES into CASH now while prices are at such a high level. I am an antique dealer's agent representing reliable and established antique dealers.

I will call back tomorrow morning.

Now what you did was this: you went to any small town or village out in the suburbs and you put a circular through the doors of about three hundred houses and you went back the next day. I normally put these circulars out on a Tuesday because, in many cases, when I called back on Wednesday, the householder might be short of cash before pay-day and want to sell something. There were other "slappers" who only dealt in gold or silver and had no knowledge of clutter or curios or books of the sixteenth or seventeenth centuries. The competition of buying gold and silver on the knocker was terrific, and I got a comfortable existence with my pamphlet because I put on the end of my pamphlet: "I want you to thoroughly understand that I not looking for gold and silver and diamonds. I'm only looking for articles that I can buy for about five or six shillings apiece."

It was hard work jumping about and going backwards and forwards, and with this type of livelihood you were also, at times, offered a lot of rubbish that was completely useless. I did very well with broken alarm clocks because I used to take a gamble on them and buy them for a shilling, and in many cases they weren't broken, they had stopped because they were dirty, and I used to clean them and get five shillings for them immediately. Some days I was lucky and I would get three or four alarm clocks, and sometimes I'd go for about a week without getting any. This was another method of getting a more or less a comfortable existence.

Round the West End there was another character—he was also a descendant of Needles, and he used to stand outside cafés and play a tune on wine glasses. When he'd finished playing a couple of tunes on his wine glasses he would imitate a lot of English birds from the forest. Occasionally he would be joined by a guitarist who would play a number and whistle the tune and while the guitarist was whistling the tune he would join in by whistling like a bird. He was married and had two children, and he was very popular amongst the Bohemians. He lived in a home-made caravan which he'd made out of an old baker's cart, and he lived in a yard in Brixton where there were other travellers' caravans. When I used to go to Brixton Market, after I'd finished, I used to pop in and have a chat with him, and he used to come up to the West End about nine o'clock at night and roam about until the early hours of the morning.

Another very lovable character who has been in the West End for at least forty years is "Gipsy Larry." He's still around now, and he always walks round with a red scarf with a gipsy cravat-ring on it, and obtains his living by playing banjo in different coffee houses. He was also one of the early pioneers of the Sun Bathers.

And there was another character by the name of "Monty" who always dressed like a down-and-out actor and wore a flowing bow tie and a large black-and-white checked jacket and had long Spanish sideboards. He lived in a cellar on The Seven Dials and wrote poetry about the underworld. I often had a chat with him—his favourite poet was Shelley—and I went down several times and had a cup of tea with him in his den, part of the wall of which he'd papered with "Editor's Regrets"[45] and these he cherished very much. All his poetry played the tune of the Jungle of Survival in the underworld. Amongst my documents I have a part of one of his poems, and it goes like this:

> Who are these haggard faces
> going in out of cafés and places
> carrying attaché cases
> all tied up with strings and laces:
> Wide boys on the floor.

He flogged his poetry round the cafés which were used by underworld characters in Rainbow Corner. And when he'd earned enough to solve his problems—which he had no difficulty in doing because he used to sell them for tuppence, and he had sheets of them—he used to drift back again to the Bohemians.

45 Presumably "rejection slips".

There was a Frenchwoman known amongst the community as "Madame." She came into Soho about fifteen years before the last World War and she dressed herself up like a Spanish gipsy with a Spanish shawl, and got acquainted with all the dives and some of the nightclubs. (At this time the two night clubs where a few Bohemians used to go were "The Silver Slipper," and "Smoky Joe's," in Gerrard Street. I met Smoky Joe on several occasions and he was a charming fellow and was very fond of Bohemians. He was also very generous. Occasionally you'd hear a character say, "I'm going round to borrow a couple of pounds off of Smoky Joe.") Madame obtained her living by selling a lucky charm made of brass which she called "The Karma Yogi": it was a very nice little idol, beautifully constructed, with a tiny hole on the top of its head so it could be hung on a chain. And she used to sell this for half-a-crown. She had the sole rights of the manufacture of it and she had no difficulty in selling it not only to the Bohemians but also to the tourists (who she would sometimes take for a tour of what she called "The Underworld.") She had a studio in Bloomsbury and she asked me to go out to see if I could get her a very nice brass Buddha. So I went perusing round the antique shops until I found one for three pounds in an antique shop in Church Street, Kensington. This was also another quarter where I used to go perusing round every fortnight. I also used to visit the British Museum about once a month but I was only interested in the top floor where they had the Oriental Department and the Tibetan curios. One afternoon I took Madame round there and after we left she said: "I've put the Buddha into a shrine. Come round to the studio and have a look at it." So I went round there and the walls of her studio were draped with desert blankets in all different coloured stripes, and she had on one part of the wall a quantity of swords and fencing masks. In her early days she'd been very interested in the art of fencing, and she showed me an album of hers with a collection of photographs of herself in her early days when she was fencing.

She was of Irish descent, half Irish and half French, and she had lived in Rome for some time before she came over here. I asked her whether she had any gipsy relations, and she said that she had a granny and a grandfather who travelled about in a caravan in France and got their living hawking in the villages. I spoke to her in one or two Needie words and she only understood about four, but I was convinced that she was a Needie because they had plenty of Needies on the Continent wandering about, as well as gipsies. She went to Paris with a young artist she met about four or five years before the last World War.

Out of all the hundreds of Bohemians that were around there was only about ten who could speak any Romany and about thirty who could speak the Jogars Polary.

While all this was going on the vagabonds and the tramps in the West End in those days were playing mouth-organs or singing in the gutters for coppers. Some were selling matches and pencils and copies of *Old Moore's Almanac*. In the early hours of the morning the wealthy classes, who had come out of the night clubs sometimes were to be seen round the coffee stalls. They were usually very generous treating the less fortunate to cups of tea and cakes and packets of Woodbines.

In those days everybody believed in liberty and life for everyone, especially the pursuit of happiness—a Utopia in existence. One section of the Bohemian community were discussing and debating and fighting as hard as they could, including myself, to try and bring this dream of a Utopia, in this mechanical civilization, into a reality. And Beauty, Music, Literature, Art and Philosophy were no longer the property of a selected few. We had forced it, with our activities, into the mind of the community. Everybody was willing to do some work amongst this crowd of people, but they weren't willing to work all day.

Round about this period, a book came out and it was entitled *The Ragged Trousered Philanthropists*;[46] I've forgotten the name of the author, but the book still floats about. And another famous book which was always being quoted and was read very widely, was called *Children of the Dead End* by Patrick MacGill.[47] This was an autobiography of an Irish navvy who worked on big building sites and it was very humorous and also rather sad, but it was very popular. Another book which I remember that was written at this period was *My First Two Thousand Years*, by 'The Wandering Jew'.[48] These books were also popular with the underworld and all the characters who frequented Hyde Park (along with *The Martyrdom of Man* which I have already mentioned). In my spare time, when I gave up speaking on the platform, I used to go up to Hyde Park to get into group discussions on the ground and I was always quoting these books. They were all obtainable from bookshops unlike Ingersoll's *Essays* or Volney's *Ruins of Empire* (both of which I also liked to quote from). These you could only consult by having a Reader's ticket for the British Museum which was too

46 Robert Tressell (1870–1911). First published in an abridged form by Grant Richards Limited in 1914.
47 Sub-titled: *the autobiography of a Navvy*. London: H. Jenkins, 1914.
48 Sub-titled: *the autobiography of the Wandering Jew* by George Sylvester Viereck (1884–1962) and Paul Eldridge. New York: The Macaulay Co., 1928.

complicated for anybody unless they had the leisure to go there and the economic security not to have to worry about where the next meal was coming from.

Now we'll jump out of the life in the West End and back again into the life on the fair grounds. What you see in the fair grounds to-day is not what you could have seen forty years ago. Show people were always on the alert for picking up freaks of nature or some kind of an interesting illusion. And there was some very interesting freaks of nature travelling about the fair grounds in these days. They exhibited "The Ugliest Woman in the World"— which was quite genuine and no fake, and they exhibited "Andy the Fish"—this was a fellow that was born with two stumps that were in the shape of fins. There was "The Legless and Armless Woman"—the last time I saw her exhibited was at Southampton on the Common. Also a very, very fat woman was exhibited; a "Tattooed Lady"—she was tattooed from head to foot, barring her face—and a really tiny dwarf, which I last saw at Nottingham Goose Fair. There were also lion tamers on fair grounds who went into the lion's cage which was only the size of a large caravan. Then there was the "Lion-Faced Boy"—who was found on the Continent and a "Lion-Faced Lady"—they both had beards like manes on their faces.

It was about twenty years ago when I met Montana Bill. This character had long hair, and had in his younger days been in America with a circus, and he used to do a sharp-shooting act. The last time I saw him was at St. Giles' Fair, Oxford. The last time I saw him performing was when he came to London. He didn't have any caravan then and he was sleeping in his sideshow. He would split an apple in half on top of his wife's head.

When he was living on the fair ground at Stratford I used to go down to see him at weekends, and it was there that I met Paul.

Paul had been, in his younger days, a merchant seaman, and he'd been to South America and he'd got friendly with Indians when he was out there and learned how to do fire-blowing with paraffin oil. I got very friendly with him, and when Montana Bill left Stratford, and went on the road to travel, I brought Paul back to my studio, and occasionally I would go out with him and introduce him to the crowd when he did his fire-eating act. He could take a mouthful of paraffin oil and he could blow a flame about twenty-five feet in length and he also used to go all over his bare flesh with burnt tapers, and he did a little bit of rope-spinning with a lasso and cracking a few stock-whips—I used to hold a piece of paper in my mouth and he used to slash it in half with a stock-whip. He had some nice props: like the Indian head-dress he wore which drew quite a nice crowd. Paul travelled all over the country in the summer-time and slept out in a sleeping-bag making a living doing his fire act. He would also do a bit of wire-working (he used to make very nice jewellery out of old gold wire) and on some occasions he would go and travel with a circus. He was a very peculiar character because he was very interested in the Mormon religion and considered himself a Mormon. I read several pamphlets on the Mormon religion, and the opinions of Brigham Young, which were sent to him from America. It might have fascinated some people, but it didn't fascinate me. However, we didn't get into any arguments about his belief and I always considered him a personal friend of mine and not just an acquaintance. I saw him just before the last World War, but I haven't seen him since.

At this period of existence it was not easy to get onto a show ground unless you were in the Showman's Guild. However, there were one or two showmen who were in the Guild—and I was not—who would allow me to travel with them. At Exeter there was a Strong Man who could lift a carthorse off the ground with his shoulders and, at a fair in Thame, there was a Strong Man who had stones broken on his chest with a sledge-hammer. There were some very interesting Posing Shows on the road in these days; they were called "Paris by Day" and "Paris by Night." The girl models who used to pose in these shows were always very beautiful and knew the art of posing. There were Illusion Shows, and there was a show where a character was hand-cuffed and chained and he escaped from a packing-case which was on the stage. All the secrets of this type of escaping I knew, but I didn't take this on because it didn't appeal to me as a career.

In these days if you were working with a side-show the fair ground opened at about midday and you went right on till twelve o'clock in the night. So whatever you earned was very, very hard-earned because then you had to pack up the show, if you were in a market-place, and get ready to go on to the next town. Once you got in with show people they were very, very friendly. But they keep to themselves—show people's friends are mostly only show people, and although they occasionally visit the West End they're not altogether fascinated by a cosmopolitan life.

For the last forty years, however, freaks of nature and sensational performing side-shows have not been seen on fair grounds.

Jinny, my wife, did perform in a Posing Show on Blackheath one year, and also did her posing act on Southampton Common one August Bank Holiday. At that time we were working for Rose Foster, the "Armless and Legless Lady", on half-share of what was taken after expenses were deducted. (In those days most show people would allow you to work for them on a percentage of the takings.) I was exhibiting my wife Jinny, in a Posing Show, at the back of "The Horse Shoe" public house in Tottenham Court Road, which was a fair ground before the picture palace was built there. Jinny was a delightful model because she had modelled at various art schools, and the show which I originated for her to pose in I called "The Exposure of an Opium Den." This performance took place in a big picture-frame, and I just drew the curtain away and exhibited for a minute the various poses. The first pose was "Temptation" and the second pose was playing with the pipe and it was called "Desire." The next pose was "Attempt" where she was playing with a box of opium pills. The next, "Wonder," she was sitting on the settee putting one of the opium pills in the pipe. Then followed "Yawning" and "Remorse" which had her asleep on the couch. We also had a short series of poses: one was called the "Venus de Milo" and another "Psyche at the Bath—Before and After the Bath." And then she went round the crowd and she sold them a photograph of herself which was autographed. The charge for this performance was thruppence.

What I've told you about are past memories—twenty years ago or more. The fair grounds of to-day have become completely modernized and they've lost the romance and the colour of the old days.

CARAVAN CLUB & AFTER-EFFECTS

Now there were little groups of people, Bohemians, in the West End who were forming different circles, and I turned away from going out with my Numerology board, as far as I possibly could. The Indians were blending a very fascinating perfume which was called "Russian Aura". For about a year I got a very, very comfortable living flogging this perfume and then I decided to sell a bottle of perfume for sixpence and to give a reading of Numerology, free of charge. I jumped about all over the place to different markets and did very well.

There was a little bit of a revival. More visitors were coming to the West End, the Caledonian Market was packed to suffocation on Tuesdays and Fridays, and money started to flow a little bit more into the hands of the Bohemians.

Now this is where I prove that decision determines, to a great extent, the destiny of a character. In my mind I had the idea of opening a colossal Bohemian night club. I also looked over what the consequence might be. What I was actually longing to do was to buy a caravan and a pony and give up my Bohemian life in London and take to the open road, but financially I didn't have quite enough capital to accomplish the feat. I was in a position where I could have got a cart, and I could have made some kind of a poor gipsy's caravan and buy a pony and some harness. I was getting a little bit weary of it all, because there was no reform taking place in society; conditions were not getting better for the working class; the Means Test was being applied to people who were destitute and the Public Assistance was allowing them just about enough money to live on bread and margarine. The characters who fiddled for an existence found things tightening up. Clutter, even at the Caledonian Market, was becoming dearer. This was because the antique dealers at the sea-side, and in the country, were getting short of commodities so these dealers were going up to the Caledonian Market and were buying all they could get hold of, probably to put by and store.

However, we could have taken to the road, Jinny and I, with a poor gipsy caravan and all our problems would have been solved, because I would have had no rent to find for a studio and we could have both fiddled about the best way we could and have got enough money to buy food and coal for the caravan.

Now this situation was determined by our decision. It was us, Jinny and I, who decided the next event and the next situation. Had I come to the conclusion, or had Jinny come to the conclusion, that we would take to the road in a caravan, and sell up what we had in the studio, there would have been no Caravan Club, and there would have been no biography of my life by Mark Benney, and probably there would have been no memoirs by me because I'm quite sure that I would have had no desire to write anything. However, the Caravan Club went into operation, and so far as I was concerned it was a colossal calamity. The consequences caused my biography to be written. This was going to produce, according to the publishers, enough royalties for me to buy a nice caravan—in those days you could get a beautiful caravan for a hundred pounds, with all the comforts you desired in it; a place which could become your home for the rest of your life. However, the last World War knocked all the royalties on the head that were due to me, and so far as I was concerned what financial assistance I achieved out of *What Rough Beast?* was nothing.

The only mental achievement was that it was a good education for the sociologists because the complete trial of the Caravan Club at the Old Bailey was portrayed in the book. The disaster of the Caravan Club sent me for a holiday in Wormwood Scrubs for a year and three months, and all my dreams were shattered as a result of me making a wrong decision. I suffered.

H. G. Wells reviewed the book and said that he didn't know whether I was a "discovery or a creation" and he said the book was "a very fine education." *The Daily Herald* in their summing-up of the book said about me that "under a better ordered society he might have been a great man." All this didn't stimulate me as I had no desire to be great or to be hero-worshipped; the only desire I ever had, is to solve the problem of existence in comfort and not to have a lot of responsibility on my shoulders. Some of the letters which I wrote to Jinny when I was in prison are in the book, as is my poem "Not Understood." And the reason I've not gone into the details of my childhood experiences is because it's already been described in my biography.

Now there was a circle in Whitfield Street which met in a very large basement and all the walls were draped with cretonne curtains. It belonged to a young man who came from Cornwall and he was known as Joe. He was very interested in finding out what the Occult Sciences were all about and he asked me to come round there and have discussions. It wasn't a circle which was known to a great number of characters that we knew, and I used this place as my personal meeting-place for about nine months. Jinny used to come along occasionally and there was quite a nice little circle of people, about twenty-five, no more, and it's here I was introduced to my partner. I won't mention his name because it's in my biography.[49] He had inherited a little bit of money. I also had a little bit of money from selling bottles of perfume and had asked Jinny to put a little aside. Another character, who had the Mauve Circle studio, had a small income for life but he was not interested in going into any business or operating in any way in England; he was thinking of going to New Zealand and settling there, which he eventually did. But between my partner and him we discussed the possibilities of the most sensational and the most exotic Bohemian night club that had ever been seen. I had quite a nice collection of fantastic curtains and about twelve benches and three or four divan settees. The rest of the paraphernalia which would be needed to put this club into operation could be bought in the Caledonian Market. At this period there happened to be a lot of Oriental curtains about, and I bought six terrific big curtains, about twelve feet in length, of black canvas and on them were painted Chinese dragons. Then we bought some canvas which had at one time been the backdrop of a theatre, and we also managed to get hold of some second-hand theatre curtains in mauve velvet. We got all this junk round into the yard of the Mauve Circle and we started having discussions how we would organize and decorate the premises when we got them.

There was a very helpful estate agent by the name of Solly who had offices in Greek Street and was well-known among the Bohemians. With his help a lot of Bohemians managed to get empty cellars and empty basements which they turned

49 He was a 24-year-old "youth" by the name of Billy Reynolds, who, it was later revealed, already had 4 convictions to his name. At the trial he was sentenced to 12 months.

Ironfoot displaying his biography in 1945.

into studios. After about three weeks we had a letter from him to say he had premises that we could look at in Endell Street; the rent was thirty shillings a week. He offered to deal with all the technical details between the landlord and the lease and the solicitors, and arrange everything.

So we went round and saw these premises. They were at 81 Endell Street, W.C.2, and the entrance was in a courtyard. It was about twenty-five feet across and about fifty feet long. We notified about ten of the Bohemian artists to come and have a look at it and assist us to decorate it, and we took the premises. My partner went and arranged for two gas stoves to be put in and we organized a kitchen; we had no bar—the sandwiches and the snacks came through a square door in the wall.

We called it the "Caravan Club" and it took us about three weeks to get the place ready. I got all the Chinese tapestries up and the velvet curtains. On the piece of canvas—which was about eighteen feet in length and twelve feet high—I got an artist to draw three or four gipsy caravans camping on a piece of ground, with a fire going by the side of the caravan, and about five gipsy women and three gipsy men sitting round in a circle. (I was sorry to lose this bit of scenery—somebody pinched it after the raid.) We subdued the lights and floodlit the ceiling, stained the floor black and threw all kinds of Indian and Chinese rugs and carpets on the floor. We had four girls down there who for three weeks were making cushions out of a very beautiful collection of colourful material; they made about sixty in all which we scattered about the place. The little low tables, about three feet high, we made out of timber. As you came in the door, and turned to the left, we had the dance floor. We had no ordinary orthodox band. The band was called "The Gipsy Band" and consisted of an accordion, two guitars, a balalaika and some tom-toms.

Well, we were messing about and organizing the place for about six weeks before we decided to open. In the meantime we had a pamphlet published and distributed. This is what it had on it:

"The Caravan"

81 Endell Street, W.C.2
(Entrance in Court)

Dear Friend,

This is to tell you that at last the dream of all lovers of literature, music, art and philosophy has become a reality.

A place for Bohemians and those in sympathy with them, having atmosphere, decorations, historical associations and comfortable, albeit artistic, seating and apartments has been established in London.

The Caravan sets out on its journey on Saturday, the 14th July, 1934, and has been and will continue to be described as the most unconventional spot in town.

Do join us there and forget for a time the ties and responsibilities that do hedge us around.

Any time between 6 p.m. and 3 a.m. we shall be happy to see you.

Abyssinia,
Prof. Jack Neave, L.P.A.

About six years previous to this all-in wrestling had become very popular and one or two all-in wrestlers had used Bohemian rendezvous and become very friendly with us. I recall Karl Karinsky and another famous wrestler by the name of Walters. When I told them I was opening a place they said they'd all come along to ensure that there wasn't any nonsense.

We took a taxi down to the Embankment one night and we rounded up some tramps and asked them if they could do a turn or make a speech or something, and we'd give them a pound and their supper. We managed to get hold of five tramps (I shall never forget that night!) and we brought them along and we put them in the cabaret. One of the tramps, who was about sixty, had done a little bit of variety and he sang a song which fitted into the situation nicely: "I Haven't Any Gold to Leave When I Grow Old, When I Leave the World Behind Me." Another did what he called the "Club Dance." The third sang "If You Were the Only Girl in the World and I Were the Only Boy." The fourth one said that all he could do was to tell us about some of his experiences. The other old boy put his tin cans and his paraphernalia in a bundle in a corner and did a very amusing dance. There was a male ballet dancer who wore tights with silver cloth leaves sewn on them and he did a peculiar dance which he called "The Dance of Remorse." We were always on the lookout for turns that were very unusual, and at that time, down by Leicester Square, it was called "Poverty Corner", where all the down-and-out actors used to hang around, trying to get work. I discovered these two girls who did what they called "Shadow Dances," which consisted of tap-dancing for about a minute and then holding the pose. On several occasions I did a turn myself. When I performed in the Caravan Club I always put on a ginger wig, blackened my eyebrows and painted my nose red.

The staff that were employed in the Caravan Club were looked after very well, and on top of that they were making, at least, a pound a night in tips. The girls were dressed in black trousers, yellow blouses and red silk handkerchiefs; the waiters were dressed in black trousers and yellow shirts and red ties. I was dressed in a velvet jacket, striped trousers and a tapestry waistcoat, and my partner had a dark mauve dinner jacket made.

There were Lords and Ladies I could mention who, on different occasions, were in my company and in with the Bohemians, but had no desire to bring their names into the limelight. I won't go into details about the trial because it is all in my biography, but however, the investigating officers got in possession of the Visitor's Book of the Caravan Club which contained two thousand names, many of them high and respectable people. There were several people in the raid who had no charge preferred against them and were discharged. There was a Spanish dancer we wanted to give a demonstration of her dance at the Old Bailey, but she wasn't allowed to do so.[50] There were several very well-known barristers in the trial and I was represented by Derek, Sir Curtis-Bennett, then Mr. Curtis-Bennett. There were over a hundred and fifty people present during the raid. A hundred and four were charged with 'aiding and abetting' of which seventy-six were discharged. But the remainder were remanded for an appearance at the Old Bailey. It was all over the newspapers and caused a terrific sensation.

50 This was a professional dancer called Carmen Fernandez. Her suggestion that she give a demonstration of the Rumba in court was not looked upon with approval by the judge Mr Henry Holman Gregory K.C.! "She Was Asked to Dance the Rumba in Court", *The Daily Mirror*, October 25, 1934, p. 8.

It was a big place and there were one or two in there who had had their cards marked by the law previously, but the thing was on such a gigantic scale I couldn't go up to everybody and ask them who and what they were. There was no sensational political news at the time and the press had nothing to scream about so this came in very useful for them because there were M.P.s there, doctors and lawyers and writers and composers and one or two characters who'd drifted in from the underworld. And the dances that took place were exaggerated in the press. It might have been more serious for me if I hadn't put up a terrific speech in the witness-box. What the jury couldn't understand was why people wanted to lead this peculiar, cosmopolitan life. In a very, very short time the fame of the Caravan Club reached right across London. And my own personal criticism of the proceedings was that it was a liberty that they made it look as black as they possibly could. My friend got twelve months and I got eighteen although nobody pleaded guilty. There was nothing to plead guilty for—the fire dance could be seen on any fair ground—and the fat man, whose dancing they kicked up such a fuss about, happened to be Solly, the estate agent, who let us the premises!

I was rather surprised to see how antagonistic they were towards me because we had a commissionaire in uniform in the place and he was from the Corps of Commissionaires. They asked him during the trial whether he saw anything which he considered was "liable to corrupt the morals of His Majesty's subjects" and he said no, he didn't see anything he would consider was not correct.

The trial was plastered all over *The News of the World* and all the other leading Sunday papers. They didn't ask the M.P. what he thought about the Caravan Club, and they didn't even ask any of the respectable people, who were discharged without a stain on their character. They did everything in their power to blacken the evidence against my partner and me. Anybody who reads an account of the trial to-day would surely come to an entirely different conclusion to what they came to in those days.

However, that was the end of the Caravan Club. There were no serious lectures given there and no discussions about the Occult—every night was Variety Night, and what made the place more popular than anything was that anybody could get up and do a turn, no matter who they were.

In the crash I lost everything. I lost scenery which belonged to me because my money went into the decoration and my partner's money went into organizing the catering. When I got out of prison nobody knew where my curtains were; nobody knew where my beautiful big incense burner, which I hung from the middle of the ceiling, had gone. At one side wall I had five exotic primitive masks, which I cherished because they'd been hanging up in my studio in Robert Street for some time, and there was a couple of very large Indian curtains studded with little tiny bits of mirror...all gone! And by the side of the floor in the dance hall my Burmese chair which was all carved with dragons—probably at some time or the other it had been brought out of a pagoda—was also missing. And several other items, many of which I cherished, had been spirited away. As a matter of fact I did not salvage a thing— neither could I find out who'd taken possession of these items. (I've often thought to go down to Scotland Yard and have them give me a photograph of the interior of it, because unless you saw a photograph of how this place was decorated you could hardly believe it.)

Now as I have said before, I blamed society and the system I lived under for the collapse of the Caravan Club and how I was treated at the trial. But I thought it over and came to the conclusion that I had no right in blaming society because society had nothing at all to do with it. They had no say in the matter, neither the possessing class, the middle class, nor the working class—these were the people who assisted me to get my living, so why should I blame them? My knowledge of the study of Dynamic Cosmology had given me a better understanding than to reason in that particular direction. This theory explains the operation of Karma, mental and physical activities, and it explains the sequence of events. It aims to alert you to the fact that whatever mental and physical action you put into operation, you should always be aware, as far as possible, of what the sequence is going to produce. So how could I blame people for something that they did not partake in? How could the rising generation be blamed for the situation? How could they be responsible for the situation that had been created by their forefathers? How could the next generation be responsible for a situation which is now being created by the existing generation? I went into the details of the situation from every angle and blamed myself for creating such a state of events. I blamed myself for creating the situation by taking the decision—my own personal decision—leaving myself open to a section of the community to take the attitude which they did towards me.

I came out of prison in March 1936. While I was inside my wife Jinny had been working behind a bar in a café, and I had a little bit of money, which I managed to put by while the

Caravan Club was operating. Jinny had still kept on the studio and her girl-friends had visited her every night and prevented her from becoming despondent. We'd lived at this studio in Robert Street for twenty years but we only rented it. So it was about time we started thinking about obtaining a shelter which we could call our own which neither the law, nor anybody else, could take away from us. If the landlady who owned the house decided to sell—well, the new tenants would probably want us to get out of the studio and, unless we had a little bit of money behind us, we would have been in a very complicated situation. (As it happened, just before the last World War the landlady *did* eventually sell the house, but by that time we had already moved to a studio at the top end of the Caledonian Road—which was only five shillings a week, unfurnished.) We sold some of our belongings and the idea was to either get possession of a small cottage or else a caravan or a houseboat.

During this period I decided to entirely disinterest myself from possessing any more social clubs. I was occasionally approached by famous people who wanted to finance me to open something similar again, but after my experiences at the trial of the Caravan Club I'd lost all interest. As a matter of fact I wouldn't have had one as a gift, I wouldn't have had even a café given to me as a gift. And this was a good thing because it changed my attitude. I didn't lose interest in the Bohemians—I could never lose interest in them—but I did lose complete interest in orthodox, conventional society and I said to myself, "Let them amuse themselves as they will."

Now the competition during the course of these years so far as horoscopes were concerned, that was finished; as was perfume. As for fiddling about with clutter, that was very difficult—you could only just get enough out of that to buy food with, and fair grounds had more or less had it—the entertainment that was taking the grip of the public at this period more than anything was dog-racing. Everybody was going to dog-racing, except the Bohemians, who were still going to their different rendezvous, as usual.

What was going on in the West End was this: there was no big meeting-place for the Bohemians so they were visiting all kinds of little dives in and round Charlotte Street. The place which I mostly visited after the collapse of the Caravan Club was a little Bohemian café down in a cellar in Charlotte Street that was open all night, called "The Cauldron." There was another small place which held about thirty people and that was also in a basement down Rathbone Place, and coming up from the door you could see the famous pub of that time, which was The Marquis of Granby.

There was a character by the name of "Snuffy" and he used to get his living in market-places by selling a lucky charm and giving tips; he was well acquainted with literature, and in his younger days had been a Needie and he'd also been a "mush faker." Now "mush faking" is repairing broken umbrellas, and in the winter-time he could survive by going round the suburbs and mending umbrellas. He could also repair cane chairs and carpets, which was known as "tiger hunting." And the material which he extracted from his occult studies, which he attached more importance to than anything else, was the Science of Vibrations. He was called "Snuffy" because he always carried a silver snuff box and when he met you, he'd always offer you a pinch of snuff. He had a little short beard and long side-boards and never wore a hat; he was rather a striking personality, a very humorous type of character—he was always jolly and he had the temperament of a Needie, which is to say he had trained himself to enjoy what one section of the community would consider as "poverty." He was always talking about Vibrations, and he had a basement in Drummond Street, by Euston Station, which he called his "Temple." He used to perform a ritual with incense sticks which he called "The Laws of Vibration." He performed this in front of a peculiar pentagram, which he'd drawn himself, saying "I am now burning incense to various reformers who have actually done something which was an asset to humanity." And one evening he took me round to his Temple, which was covered in a variety of coloured, heavy, tapestried curtains which he'd bought up the Caledonian Market and in the corner he'd built a shrine, and in behind this he'd put this peculiar pentagram and, on a velvet stand, a crystal.

He had a small gas-ring and, when we arrived, he cooked us a very nice meal. After we had finished our meal and had a smoke he talked about Vibrations. I admired him for giving reverence to the memory of reformers. In one corner of the room he had forty or fifty umbrellas and he also had a pile of cane which he used when he went out repairing chairs in the summer-time. He was supposed to have written a short manuscript about market life and travelling about the country, but I never heard any more about it and about a year after that he took to the open road and wasn't seen again.

One of the interesting things about the Bohemian life of the West End is that although all these people recognized each other and there was a complete brotherhood amongst them—you very seldom found a Bohemian who was really skint (broke) in these days because they all knew hundreds of people, and if one had nowhere to sleep there was always someone willing to put him up for the night, and if a Bohemian didn't have the price of a meal there was always somebody who had a bit of something to give him. But the main thing is that all of this variety of people mingled together in little clubs like The Sunshine, The Last Chance, Peggy's Cellar, The Café Bleu or The Lounge. We had a complete circle of people who were bound together in a brotherhood although today only about thirty of the old-timers remain.

The all-in wrestlers met in one place, but they didn't monopolize the place completely—there were other people floating in and out. The ballet dancers used another place and the artists' models had their own place and the artists used another place and there were other places where there were little political clubs such as the ILP and the SPG and the Anarchist Groups, and all these different groups used to congregate together. The market workers would be talking among themselves and the buskers would be talking among themselves, occasionally talking to other people. The antique dealers, who fiddled about with knick-knacks, would be in a group talking to each other, and the people who fiddled in second-hand books would be talking together. The characters who slept out all night in sleeping-bags, and led more or less a vagabond life and obtaining their living by what was known as pearl-diving (washing dishes), they would never do anything but part-time work, because they only worked to get enough to survive on from day to day; they would all be in little different groups, talking together. At this time, early on at this period, there were two clubs that were visited by the "arty-arty" types and among them there were the "poseur intelligentsia" and a few characters who considered themselves to be from the underworld. The Occult Sciences, however, were never discussed in dives where all the other people congregated; they were only discussed in studios where the members were sincerely interested in finding out what they were all about.

After my release from the drama of the Caravan Club, I took it very easily for one year. I went to Brighton occasionally for a couple of days and slept out at Shoreham in my sleeping-bag, and occasionally for two or three days I would go to Oxford and I would sleep out on Port Meadow or out by the Trout Inn at Wolvercott. I could always buy ten shillings' worth of knick-knacks, curios and odds and ends in the clutter shops and I could sell them again to the trade or people who were fiddling with them on stalls and sometimes earn a pound or twenty-five shillings. I knew Saunders in the High Street, a bookshop in Oxford, and I also frequented Blackwell's where I would go up in their Occult Department and see if I could find any pamphlets or any literature on Cosmic Dynamics which, for the last thirty years, has been my favourite subject. I was often in and out of the Occult Department in Foyles and I also went in and out of Waters[51] in Cecil Court, near Leicester Square, looking for literature on Cosmic Dynamics.

But now let us get back to the interior decorations of some of the beautiful places and how they were constructed and decorated. The proscenium on the wall of The Lounge in Gerrard Street, which operated about forty years ago, took a considerable time to do and was done by a famous French artist. I'm often sorry I didn't have a photograph of it. It reached from the door right round three-quarters of the wall, and it was an oil painting of Venice—a landscape, with the boats on the

---

51 I think Jack must mean Watkins, the famous occult bookstore still in Cecil Court today.

canal and all the people in historical costumes and aristocrats riding about on horses—and it was done not as it is to-day but in an historical period. The Lounge drew an enormous amount of theatre-goers, and there were ladies and businessmen in top hats who'd come out of theatres drinking all together and talking with Bohemians. It was open till four o'clock in the morning and there'll never be a place like that again.

The Chat Noir in Old Compton Street was one of the first types of French café in London. There was a complete bar in the centre of the room shaped like an egg and the customers sat round it and the other customers sat on the side. The proprietor was very fond of prints and there was one or two Hogarths on the wall and one or two Cruikshanks, and on the rest of the wall the poor artists were allowed to hang up their paintings. These were for sale, and that helped them in obtaining a living—of course, in those days a poor artist would sell you a painting for less than a pound. The Chat Noir was really popular until Paul, the proprietor, evaporated into the elements and that was the finish of it.

The Café Bleu in Old Compton Street was the next rendezvous which was frequented and this had mural landscapes on the wall which were done with plaster of Paris mixed with common household paint but were quite nice. They were done by an Italian artist and this new quick type of landscape painting became popular in the London cafés and night clubs. The Café Bleu ran for about five years and then it collapsed.[52] They spent a lot of money reconstructing it but it became very expensive serving high-class Continental food. In the old Café Bleu you could get a good plate of spaghetti for sixpence.

52 Apparently, having survived the Blitz, it burned down in 1945 due to an electrical fault. The manager moved to Bianchi's on Frith Street next door to Bar Italia.

There was a song composer who I met in those days, and he'd turned to a Bohemian life. His father was very wealthy and owned a factory somewhere in the East End that manufactured some kind of commodity. He'd been to college, but he wasn't interested in the activities of his father's business and aspired to the Arts. He had a few hundred pounds in the bank, and lived in a studio in Chelsea, next to the Town Hall. He took me down to his studio and introduced me to some of his Chelsea friends, who were very, very arty-arty and aristocratic, and I was rather surprised at the delicious welcome that I got. In his studio he had three beautiful large Belgian tapestries on the wall. One tapestry was of a Spaniard playing a mandolin to a beautiful Spanish woman leaning over the verandah of a small Spanish castle; the second was of some Indian snake-charmers and four beautiful girls doing a Pagoda Dance. The other tapestry was of aristocrats in historical armour who were probably asking these gipsy Needies what they were doing camping on their land. The tent that they had pitched was typical of the real bow-topped historical gipsy tent and all the little pikies (that is, the children) were playing around the camp-fire with the granny of the gipsies smoking a clay pipe. To me this scene was beautifully constructed. There was also a kind of a verandah with some prayer mats hanging from the railings.

He had a Collard and Collard grand piano and he played one or two new songs to me, which he had composed, and we had a very nice chat. He then asked me whether I could give him any ideas for songs. And after doing a bit of meditating, I created two titles. One title, to which I only wrote one verse, he was going to turn into a waltz. I called it "You Found a New Toy to Play With, but It's Not Like the Toy You Broke." Then I gave him a few lines which he liked and he paid me five pounds for them:

"This world is very wide and two go side by side,
Each one a different dream, each one a different scheme
Some strive for fame and others strive for game,
But my desire is You."

Around about the period of the General Strike he came to see me in my studio in Robert Street and he told me he'd locked up his studio in Chelsea and he was going to Paris for a while.

Unfortunately, I never saw him again. I suppose he decided to live out his life there.

Then there was a very interesting character who was a craftsman and had a little second-hand shop in Hanway Street, off Tottenham Court Road. It specialized in selling brass candlesticks, trays, plaques, knockers, horse brasses and all the brass knick-knacks that you could think of. This character was getting on in years, and he was often to be seen wandering about the Caledonian Market buying-up his brass commodities. I had an idea that his forefathers had been wandering Needies because he could speak Jogars Polary. Occasionally I sold him some brass items, when I bought them at the right price. He was getting a fairly comfortable living and was more or less economically secure. In the summer-time he would invite me down to his workshop (which was underneath, in the cellar) and I was able to fiddle a few bob cleaning up some of the brass. His daughter was producing pewter pictures and framing them. It was quite simple because all you had to do was to get somebody to draw a landscape on a piece of paper and then trace it with a little bit of pressure on the back of the pewter, and the pewter was then laid on a slab of cork, and after about half an hour's careful performing with a wooden skewer you had the complete design of a landscape. Then you filled in the back impressions of the skewer with plaster of Paris and turned it over onto a piece of cardboard, which fixed the design. Then all you had to do was to frame it and you didn't require any glass. She also mounted semi-precious stones into pewter brooches. I asked her father if I could try my hand at tracing some of these pictures and he said I could. So I started to produce these pictures and this was another card up my sleeve for solving the problem of existence. About a year after that I went round to his shop one day and it was closed. I never saw him after that and supposed that this charming character had evaporated into the elements.

I was getting a comfortable existence Fridays and Saturdays with clutter on the Caledonian Market; I had more or less packed up my fiddle with my Astrology board. Jinny was occasionally doing a few hours posing at various art schools. I discovered a warehouse where I could buy sheets of lead in various thicknesses. I started whacking out Chinese dragons with a skewer on the back of these sheets and framing them in frames that I could buy at a penny or tuppence apiece. I could buy a sheet of lead a foot square for sixpence. So I used to produce about ten of these pictures in four hours, and I had no trouble in whacking them out in clutter shops and also to tourists in the various dives from a half-a-crown to four shillings apiece. Probably there's still quite a few of them, lying about to-day, which I had the pleasure of producing. And I also found a method of taking an impression of large historical medallions. I would look for plaques which were reproductions of Greek and Roman heads and reproduce these in lead. I discovered a useful warm water wax with which I filled up the cracks of the impressions made by the skewer. This saved me a lot of messing about with plaster of Paris and when it was impressed into the grooves of the lead it became much harder than the plaster of Paris; it set completely hard in five minutes and was just the thing I was looking for. I didn't let on to anybody that I was producing these lead pictures. I made it my business to see that the frames I put them in were as old as possible so they looked as if they'd been produced in the Georgian era.

And this secret about producing these lead pictures and medallions I've not divulged to anybody up to now so I've given you one of my most cherished secrets. I have other cherished secrets which I have no intention of divulging to anybody, because we still live in a more or less jungle of survival so far as trade secrets are concerned.

Another good thing occurred while I was rummaging round in clutter shops in the Midlands. I managed to get hold of a very fine brass plaque of Shakespeare and also two very fine copper plaques of Beethoven and Napoleon. So I packed up doing my landscapes and I did quite a few impressions of these onto lead. And the one that was most popular in the clutter shops was the plaque of Shakespeare. I was very careful: I only took one at a time into a clutter shop and I never went into the same clutter shop twice. And I found no difficulty in selling them for four or five shillings apiece wherever I went. I wasn't silly enough to go out with a great load of these plaques and display them all at once because they might have cottoned-on that they were the outcome of some mechanical production. Later when I was living in a cottage in Oxford I fixed up a little workshop to produce these plaques and eventually I got hold of a small plaque of George Washington. This I had no problem in whacking out to the Yanks and they used to say when I showed it to them: "George Washington! How the hell did he get here?"

It was amazing how Shakespeare and Washington sold without argument. Had I known all this thirty years ago I could have avoided a lot of unnecessary nonsense that I had to put up with, such as getting messed around by the authorities and chased all over the place when I was trying to solve the problem of existence with Numerology.

As far as my researches go, I claim that a lot of people all over the country who operate clutter shops, second-hand wardrobe shops and also small marine stores are mostly the descendants of Needies. A "marine store" is where "totters"—that is people who buy and sell rags and metal—take them and they put them on the scales and they are sold by weight. Brass, copper and lead have a trade value and the woollies—that is woollens, pullovers, anything wool—have a set trade price as does white rags and all coloured rags and coloured cloth. And there are still plenty of fiddling marine stores in the towns and villages. There's one in Oxford called Warburton's. Mr Warburton is a friend of mine who I have gone backwards and forwards to for years. When I go and see him he often has bits of tapestry or velvet curtains which he sells to me for my own personal use, not for re-sale, at the value price on the scales.

Now Jinny was Scotch. She came from the Highlands and she was brought up in Glasgow. She had brothers and sisters in Edinburgh and Glasgow. Jinny and I were both getting restless, very restless, and we both felt like travelling. We had a long discussion and Jinny said that she would like to have a look at Scotland and I said, "Well, we'll sell up and only keep the things which are essential, which we cherish, and you write a letter to your sister" (who lived in the suburbs of Edinburgh) "and you make arrangements to go to Scotland for a while, and I'll jump around about Oxford and see if I can get hold of a caravan or a cottage."

The "Café Ann" (which I will describe later on) had been opened about three weeks on the High Street, Bloomsbury, by the side of St. Giles's Church. It was here that I met up with Mark Benney and we discussed writing my biography—not my memoirs, there's very little here that's in *What Rough Beast?* I went and saw the publishers, Peter Davies, and had a discussion with them and they agreed to advance me twenty pounds and a percentage of royalties on the book when it was on sale, if I'd cooperate with Mark Benney. I had a diary which I used to do regular writing in for about two or three hours a week, and I handed this diary to him and arranged to meet him in his studio in St. John's Wood. I drew the twenty pounds off of Peter Davies and went on home to Jinny, and told her that we can now put our ideas into operation.

I gave her fifteen pounds and she packed one of her cases with her belongings and she said, "Sell everything in the studio in the Caledonian Market and I'll write to you." So I got a taxi and went to Euston Station to bid her good-bye on the midnight train to Glasgow. And about four or five days after that I got a letter from her to say, "I'm in Glasgow. This is a great change for me. I can live with my sister for a pound a week, and I can also pop over to Edinburgh and see my other sister. I can also get a part-time job in a café in Glasgow." I missed her, and probably she missed me too, but in the circumstances it was the best thing we could do, as we both wanted to reorganize and we were determined to get a caravan or an unfurnished cottage and get away from furnished rooms and landladies. We didn't want to finish our days in a furnished room under the eyes of an orthodox, conventional landlady. We wanted a place of our own where we could have privacy and freedom, and the only solution to this was either a caravan, a houseboat, or a cottage.

The next week I sold everything I'd got, apart from some very important books and also some blankets, velvet curtains and tapestries. All these cherished items I packed up. I knew a gipsy, who lived in Headington, the other side of Oxford, and at the back of his bungalow, which he'd built on his own ground, he had some sheds. I asked him whether he would allow me to store my belongings in one of the sheds, and he said he would be very pleased to assist me.

A few days afterwards I got a lorry, which happened to be going in that direction, to pick my things up. It cost me about thirty shillings. I'd packed the books and the odds and ends in tea-cases and the curtains and the blankets I'd tied in bundles and I had a very, very good sleeping-bag which I cherished very much because it was supposed to have belonged to an explorer. It was padded and well-lined, and I had a double groundsheet. And so I said to myself, "Well, this is good-bye to me living in London for a while."

OXFORD

Somehow or other I felt that Oxford was my spiritual home. I'd been to St. Giles' Fair on occasions and the local population were very sympathetic towards me. There were two nice little artistic cafés in St. Ebbe's, and one or two of the local characters of the working class area of Oxford were acquainted with Literature, Art and Philosophy, and I was always welcomed in these little cafés. There was a second-hand clothes store and the proprietor was a friend of mine. He also dealt in junk and I could always sell him some junk or buy a bit of junk from him. And gipsies were occasionally to be found camping a few miles outside of Oxford and going in to get their living, and there were one or two original Needies who had little cottages in the slums of Oxford and had settled down with their families. So wherever I went north, south, east or west I could always find friends and companionship.

I stopped in Oxford for a week and camped out in one of my friend's sheds in my sleeping-bag. I'd raised twelve pounds out of a lot of antique junk I had accumulated over the years, and some books I didn't pay a lot of importance to.

I wrote a letter to Mark Benney telling him that I would be down in London for about a week at St. John's Wood to dictate some notes for my biography, and I sent Jinny a few more pounds and told her not to worry, but to content herself until I'd got in possession of either a caravan or a cottage or a houseboat. I received a letter from her every week; she'd been to see her sister and said that my niece and my nephews all sent their regards. She decided to remain with her other sister in Glasgow until I got organised.

Eventually I managed to hire a caravan on Shotover Park. It was in a rather dilapidated condition but it was a shelter from the elements and I started to live there.

Anyway, I lived in this caravan for three years whilst I was fixing up this cottage I'd found in the quarry at Headington. It had not been occupied for some years and was supposed to be condemned. There was a family living in the cottage next door to it, and it belonged to one of the relations of this dealer who I had my caravan from. I went and saw him and he said I could have it for seven-and-six a week. It contained one room twelve-by-twelve, a little room six-by-six, and a room up above it about eight-by-eight, plus another little room about six-by-six. There was a garden and a very nice large coalhouse; the water had to be drawn from a pump in the yard. So eventually I took possession of it and moved out of the caravan. But this was not until I had been living for three years in the caravan so I've got to go back two years now...

Jinny was quite contented in Scotland with her sisters and her nieces and her nephews and I was quite contented in Oxford. I used to spend four days there and three days in London.

When I wanted to go to London I would take the bus to the village of Wheatley where there was a canteen in a roadhouse made from an old railway carriage called "The Last Chance." From there I could hitch a ride on one of the lorries coming from the Midlands. So for a packet of cigarettes and a few cups of tea I could always get a lift to London. And coming back I'd sometimes get a cheap ticket from Paddington to Oxford on the workman's train at 5.30 in the morning. I had a busker friend, whose name was Fred, and he had rather a large basement in Camden Road, so I arranged that I could camp down on the floor in my sleeping-bag for a few shillings any time I liked, and I co-operated with Mark Benney in doing my biography.

At this period of my evolution I'd had a look round the warehouses in Houndsditch to see if there was any new type of interesting cheap jewellery, and there was a firm that was manufacturing a very nice bracelet, in imitation gold and imitation silver, with five charms on; these bracelets were one-and-three apiece. I bought twenty imitation silver bangles and twenty imitation gold bangles, and I discovered that I could whack these bangles out privately, and to clutter shops, for four shillings with no trouble as they seemed to suit all the artistic girls. That was two-and-nine profit on every one, and I could make from ten to fifteen bob a day jumping about quite easily; it was one of the finest lines I ever discovered.

With the surplus money I was accumulating I could run round clutter shops and I could buy, according to my judgment, little bits of Victorian jewellery which I could sell again privately for twice as much as I paid for them. With the clutter game I always worked on the system that if I paid a shilling, I wanted two for it; if I paid two shillings, I wanted four for it because there was the time and the trouble and the scrounging about to be taken into consideration. The same applied to scrounging books—if I paid a shilling I was always satisfied if I got two for it, and if paid two shillings I was satisfied if I got four for it.

By this time I had developed a very keen sense of judgment and I often wondered what a pity it was I didn't have this knowledge in the early part of my career because jumping about with an Astrology board at times became very monotonous.

I was not lonely in Oxford because I made many friends; I could sell books if they were old to Saunders bookshop in the High Street, and I could also sell books to Blackwell's. There were many good bars in Oxford and I could get a bus home up till about half-past eleven at night. There was a good café bar right next door to the theatre in Oxford where the repertory company performed. I also spent a good deal of time down in the artistic cafés of the St. Ebbe's district. I corresponded with Jinny regularly in Scotland and I had no trouble in sending her thirty bob a week and keeping myself in semi-comfort.

A year later, 1939, my biography was published and it was in all the bookshops in Charing Cross Road and the West End, and it did cause a great sensation amongst market workers, show people and the Bohemians of the West End—and the first issue was sold out in about a month. The publicity that it got was terrific and in some of the write-ups there were all kinds of controversies.

When I was in London I used the Café Ann for lounging about in and meeting people at night. The Café Ann's paintings were done by an artist and they were more or less cartoon portraits consisting of women and men who were outstanding characters in the West End, including one of me and also quite a quantity of political cartoons. There was a billiards saloon underneath the café which attracted more characters of the underworld than it did Bohemians.

There was a character by the name of Walloby who created a new society which was called the "Society of Ideology" and it had a weekly magazine which was sent to its members. I read the first one and enjoyed it very much, because this school of scholars no doubt waded into a good quantity of literature that was appertaining to curious learning, and they not only gave lectures on various ideologies but they attempted to explain them, and this was a subject I was most interested in: the Cause and the Effect. Most journals wrote articles about the effects and they didn't bother about dealing with the causes. I became a member of this society, and they had a meeting-room in a building round the back of Oxford Street and I went to one and listened to the discussions and arranged to have the journal sent to me every week. It was a school of thought—human disposition and temperament—that they were trying to tackle at a different angle.

Then a year before the last World War there was a terrific lull and a kind of a depression set in of morbid apathy. A lot of characters were beginning to leave the West End and get themselves away, some to Paris. There was what I call a "Vibration", which I would explain from an Occult angle: there was a lull of stagnation. You just couldn't sell anything. Different characters that I knew were asking me to buy their pawn tickets: they were pawning everything that they could in order to survive. So I went back to Oxford and I decided to only come up to London on a Saturday morning and to go back to Oxford on the nine o'clock train from Paddington.

I was now living in the cottage and struggling to pay the seven-and-six rent a week. So one night I burnt some incense in the cottage to a little brass Buddha which I had on the mantelpiece. I wanted to grasp a vibration (that is, an idea) of how to solve this problem, and after meditating for about an hour I got it at last. The only solution I could think of—bearing in mind it was useless trying to sell anything—was totting.

So I jumped about the clutter shops in Oxford and managed to get hold of a good pair of wheels and I made myself a nice little cart, and I went out totting. Now I never allowed myself to look scruffy; I can't remember any time, in the last forty years, that I was not wearing a collar and a cravat. I also knew another secret, which was known by the Needies: if you didn't have a clean collar and shirt you went into any draper's shop and you asked them if they would sell you, for a couple of coppers, a large white box which they put drapery in. You then drew the design of a collar onto the box, using your own collar, and then cut it out very carefully. With the other side of the white box you made yourself a front. Now I don't think the population of Oxford had ever seen anybody with a velvet jacket and tapestry waistcoat and a clean collar and a cravat, with a nice scarf laid on, knocking at the door asking them if they had any old rags to sell or dented pewter teapots. I was surprised myself when I went round all the working-class and upper-class homes to find the citizens to be quite sociable towards me and not at all antagonistic. Having a great knowledge of ideology, I thought that they had come to the conclusion that I was an artist who had gone off my rocker. Somehow my beau camaraderie, the way I spoke to them, rather fascinated them. I didn't make it my business to go to the front door of the big houses, I always went to the side door; and I was not completely broke and could afford to pay for my metal and my rags. But I did not ask them if they had any old iron or bones, and I wasn't interested in copper or brass and lead because I had been to Walburtons, the marine store, and he said he'd give me a good price only for pewter and the standard price for my rags.

This involved me walking three or four miles a day and out of this performance I managed to earn between thirty shillings and two pound a week. I could feel myself losing the desire for London. I had the addresses of about fifty of my friends, and I wrote to them asking them not to let anybody know where I was. And they all explained in their letters that a very serious situation was developing. The Café Ann was gradually "going on the floor"—that is: going broke. A lot of little dives in the West End had closed up and the proprietors had got their skates on in different directions, and an enormous amount of characters had done the same. In the Caledonian Market there were great big patches of unoccupied ground, where the clutter people used to throw their clutter out on the slabs, and a lot of stall-holders, especially antique dealers, were ceasing to use the market. And the vibrations that were going around at this time, so far as I was concerned, was a warning to me that there was either going to be a political explosion or some kind of a terrific crash.

I listened to the wireless in one or two of the saloon bars in the pubs in Oxford, and one tune they were playing was called "Stormy Weather" and the other tune was entitled "I'm Heading for the Last Roundup."

There were very few of the clutter shops, antique shops or even bookshops doing any business. I got plenty of good second-hand clothes amongst my rags—trousers, jackets, waistcoats and overcoats, and instead of taking these half-decent clothes to the rag stores I sold them to the local navvies (the workers who were working on buildings round about St. Ebbe's) who gave me a little bit more for them than I could get on the scale in the rag store. Also, I used to collect together all my newspapers in a pile and sell them to a butcher's and a fish shop in the village of Headington. In the quarter where the little artistic cafés were there were some very lovable characters who were local residents; and down this end of Oxford there were several streets of little cottages. The people who were in a better position in life looked upon them as slums, but you can enjoy paradise in a so-called slum if the rent is only five or six bob a week; and I knew a lot of these characters very, very well, and occasionally there were some that went out poaching for rabbits. There was a butcher's about a quarter of an hour's walk from my cottage and I managed to persuade him to sell me six penn'orth of block ornaments (that is, little bits of meat) twice a week; I also managed to get in with one or two grocer's shops in Oxford where you could get a pile of cheese rinds for sixpence.

There were about three local totters who were residents of Oxford and had been totting for a lifetime, and when they saw I was totting they were not antagonistic to me. They treated me like one of their own; they didn't know exactly who I was and they accepted me as a travelling totter who had just arrived in town and decided to settle for a while.

And then the great calamity was approaching. Some date in September of the next year war was declared,[53] and I turned it over in my mind and I thought to myself: what a terrible thing this mechanical civilization is. They're going to throw iron foundries at one another. To think that after years of culture and debating, coaxing and persuading and building hospitals, and doing everything in their power to bring about some kind of a more humane and a more civilized society, they're going to perform with bombers in the air.

53 September 1, 1939.

The night war was declared I walked and lounged on the roundabout at Headington till about one o'clock in the morning. It was a blackout night and there were hundreds of cars using the roundabout to evacuate wives and children in all different directions.

I didn't come up to London. I had a letter from a friend in London who told me they'd closed the Café Ann and nearly all the Bohemian dives. Bohemians had got their skates on and left whilst the ones that were getting on in years had joined the Home Guard or the Fire Guard. The Caledonian Market was closed and there was a barrage balloon flying over it.

The great City of Oxford, the city of learning and dreaming spires, was throwing its shadows across Port Meadow and there was a stillness of silence in the blackout; the cars on the roads had all their headlights dimmed.

I was so shocked with the situation that I couldn't attempt to try and get a living for at least another fortnight. I still had a little bit of money by me which I nursed very carefully, so I was in a position to pay the rent of this cottage for a few months in advance and all I had to worry about was doing a bit of fire-watching and fiddling about for food. A very short time after this the rationing of food came in, and I got a letter from Jinny, four days after war was declared, to say that she was not going to join me yet.

I felt this totting business was gradually coming to a standstill because there were articles in the *Oxford Mail* every other day about donating salvage for the war effort. And in about a month after war had been declared the local population of Oxford had thrown out all their rags and all the metal that they possessed. Fortunately I was lucky enough, while going around totting, to get hold of three very nice second-hand divans, and had a few blankets and sheets and I also had a quantity of heavy velvet and tapestry curtains, so there was plenty of bedding in the cottage.

I met a newspaper boy in Oxford who was a local. His name was Gerry and he was one of those characters who, when he wasn't selling newspapers, was to be found in one of these little artistic cafés at the bottom of St. Ebbe's. He had been born somewhere in the outskirts of Oxford and wandered to different industrial towns in the Midlands in his early days. He'd studied Theosophy, read Sir Oliver Lodge and Conan Doyle on spiritualism and he had also read *The Koran*, and when I met him he was reading a book called T*he History of the Rosicrucians.*[54] He was living in one of the local lodging-houses and everybody seemed to know him. At one time he pushed parcels to the railway station and also carried people's bags when they came out. He'd discovered the secret of going round butcher's shops and grocer's shops and scrounging block ornaments for a few coppers and scrounging bacon cuttings instead of buying the bacon in rashers, and also scrounging grocer's shops for cheese cuttings. And he knew the outlay of all the surrounding districts of Oxford. Although he was rather muddled up in his ideas about the Occult Sciences I liked him and never attempted to refute his ideas—which he'd come to by his own conclusions— because they stimulated him, and to me it was very humorous. He'd read so much of *The Koran* and the Persian classics (and he was always looking for anything that had been translated from the Persian into English) that he developed a very amusing

54 Probably *The Real History of the Rosicrucians* by A. E. Waite (London: George Redway, 1887, although Fr Wittemans' *A New and Authentic History of the Rosicrucians* had been published in 1938 (Chicago: Aries Press).

complex which, under the circumstances, so far as I was concerned, was quite a good attitude towards life. Now, so far as he was concerned, everything that occurred, was the "Will of Allah"—everything! And the local characters in the cafés in Oxford used to pull his leg very, very humorously and when they saw him they used to say, "It was the Will of Allah." I asked Gerry if he'd ever visited the West End and he said he'd been up there several times, and, when he came to London, he always went to the Occult Department in Foyles to see if he could find anything on Persian literature.

And there was another character there who probably was the descendant of a Needie because he could talk the Jogars Polary—and I had a chat with him and it turned out his parents were Needies who travelled about the country in home-made caravans. In the winter-time he got himself work on building sites, and he had a great knowledge of herbs. Like Gerry he lived in one of the local lodging-houses in Oxford which, probably, in days gone by, had been the local lodging-house for travelling Needies and their families. He had a suitcase, which we call a "peter", containing about fifteen books on the history of herbs. He made a study of herbs and also flowers, and in the summer-time he could take a sack and wander across the fields collecting a quantity of various kinds of herbs; and he had a place where he could sell these wild weeds and herbs which were used for making up various medicines. He was another very humorous character: never sad, never serious, and liked by all the characters in Oxford.

Occasionally college boys used to come down and have a cup of coffee and sometimes there were little discussions going on amongst the locals. One evening Gerry was sitting with me having some coffee and there'd been a lot of talk about air raids and this character—he was a very fat, stumpy little fellow with a fascinating grin—said to Gerry, "I suppose that if somebody dropped a ton of dynamite on your nut this would be the Will of Allah". And Gerry said, yes, it would be the Will of Allah. "And if somebody jumped off the top of a building, would that be the Will of Allah?" And Gerry said that, no matter what occurs, all was the Will of Allah. And the most amazing part about it was that Gerry was so convinced that everything was the Will of Allah that when the sirens went for an air raid he was calm and collected, and when everybody jumped up to dash to an air raid shelter, Gerry just sat there and took no notice at all. I had no desire to argue or discuss with Gerry and try and shatter his beliefs, because it would have been a shame. He was convinced of these beliefs and it stimulated him.

I used to ask Gerry to come to my cottage some nights and assist me to do a bit of painting and knock up a bit of home-made furniture out of timber. Within a month the cottage was made very, very comfortable.

Now seeing that nearly four months had elapsed and the local population had thrown out all their rags and all their metal there was only occasionally a few piles of papers to be bought, and these could be sold, providing they were clean, to a fried fish shop and two butchers in the village of Headington. And I was wondering what the next move was going to be.

Now apart from their huge selection of new books on the first and second floors, Blackwell's, the main bookshop in Oxford, had a colossal collection of second-hand books on different subjects. I saw the buyer, and he said the only books that they would buy right away were books on Oriental travels;

he didn't want any Continental travels of any description. So I started taking buses to the outlying villages and went backwards and forwards from Oxford scrounging the clutter shops and the bookshops that were in existence in Reading, Aylesbury, High Wycombe and Banbury for books that I could sell to Blackwell's. I could find about three books a day on travel to Oriental countries and for these I had to pay one-and-sixpence or two shillings. Blackwell's were giving me five shillings apiece for them, if they were in good condition. So after all the jumping about, and the bus fares, I was earning about eight shillings a day. Out of that I had to send ten or fifteen bob to Jinny and pay the rent of the cottage, which was seven-and-six a week, and I just about had enough to survive. I bought a very good second-hand oil stove which I could cook on, and used to take Gerry along with me to the cottage and produce a very substantial meal.

But I realized I'd have to find some better caper than this. I couldn't obtain any sheet lead in Oxford, or in any of the other towns round about, so I couldn't make any lead pictures.

After thinking for two or three days of every game under the sun I found the solution to the problem at last. The next thing to be put into operation was to have a pamphlet published offering high prices for disregarded clutter and miscellaneous antiques. I had the pamphlet printed and this started me back on a game which I'd operated before.

I got the pamphlets and went to a second-hand jeweller's shop in the market. The owner said he wanted all the second-hand wrist watches, clocks and alarm clocks I could get hold of, no matter what condition. So I started going out every day on a bus to the surrounding districts and villages and I was giving two shillings for broken clocks, watches and alarm clocks no matter what condition they were in. And there were quite a quantity of broken watches and clocks to be collected and I discovered that by this method, after I'd deducted the money that I'd laid out to buy these items, that I could earn, comfortably, from ten to fifteen bob, sometimes a pound a day. I doubled Jinny's money again to thirty bob, and I looked after Gerry—I saw he always had a good substantial banquet in my cottage. He wasn't on a regular pitch selling papers—he was walking round selling the *Oxford Mail*—so was only earning six or seven shillings a day. He also had a little game, which got him a few shillings in the winter, as he used to go round the covered-in market in Oxford and collect all the empty orange boxes and sell them for firewood. But all this was "The Will of Allah" so he was happy.

While I was perusing round in a clutter bookshop in Reading's London Road, I found a nice copy of *The Koran* which had coloured plates, and I also found a nice copy of the poems of Omar Khayyam and some manuscripts that were written in Persian. I didn't know what these manuscripts were about but I bought them and presented them to Gerry as I thought he would cherish them. He not only cherished them, he practically worshipped them! That night I made a terrific stew: a "gipsy's soup". It contained sausages and bacon and meat and barley and rice and onions and carrots and beans and peas and about a pound of dried fruit. I managed to obtain a very large saucepan and I made this soup which Gerry and I really enjoyed. There was no electric light in the cottage and there was no gas, but I had a candelabra which held four candles. I also had a little Buddha on the mantelpiece and a little brass figure of the God of Plenty. I had hung some mauve velvet curtains all around the walls of the cottage and placed some orange boxes on top of one another with a few books in. When I put the blackout curtain up, Gerry said, "we'll now have a Ritual."

I shifted the table into the backyard, and Gerry put his prayer carpet on the floor—and he put a little Buddha on one side of these manuscripts and the little brass God of Plenty on the other side, and his incense sticks in the incense burner, and he read out of *The Koran* some of his favourite verses. I sat on an orange box with some cushions on it and had a nice smoke, and we had a Ritual for about an hour. He read about ten verses out of *The Koran* then knelt on the floor at the end of the carpet and let his head touch the middle of the carpet, and waved his hands about, saying, "Everything, everything in the Universe, no matter what happens, good or bad, is the Will of Allah!" I liked Gerry very, very much because his loyalty was so sincere and I was sorry for him because he had no friends. He was a complete lone wolf. Nobody understood him—all the locals used to think that he was completely off his rocker. I asked him what conclusions he'd come to when he'd read the Rosicrucians, and he said he couldn't find any Christian faith, of any description, which made any impression on him at all. However, we had a very enjoyable evening and he stopped that night in the cottage.

A year elapsed, and I received several letters from London, and also from different parts of the country, from friends who knew where I was. I also corresponded with my friend Bill every week. When he came up to Oxford, every six weeks or so, we used to meet another friend Bill—who was working at pearl-diving and sweeping-up in the Mitre Hotel—and spend an enjoyable weekend together. Bill from London would stay over at my cottage for the weekend and go back to London on the Monday morning.

About a year later Jinny arrived from Scotland and straight away I noticed something very, very peculiar about her. She wasn't delighted to see me, she was in a depressed mood, and didn't want to talk about her sisters and her friends in Glasgow and didn't want to discuss anything about the war. She had no desire to go anywhere, not even to the pictures. Eventually I got hold of a second-hand wireless set for her, a battery set, and this she used to like to listen to. But when the news came on about what was going on in the war, she'd turn it off: she didn't want to listen to that. And although she was the same Jinny, physically, she was not the same Jinny mentally. She wasn't concerned about what I was doing or what I had done. As a matter of fact, she wasn't concerned about me at all. Fortunately she met one of the local women, who was working in the car works, and got very friendly with her. I was very, very pleased because, all her life, Jinny enjoyed the company of women (she was always on about their emancipation). This woman's husband was a very nice chap; he was a local, and he was a descendant of one of the generations of the village. She had a meal ready for me when I came home and then this woman would either come round and join Jinny for a few hours, or Jinny would go round to her cottage and join her—and it seemed to me that the less she saw of me, the better.

I carried on my routine for another year and then Jinny decided to go up to the works with this woman and she got herself a job up there in the canteen. She didn't change her attitude, and she said that she didn't want to be annoyed by me so I decided to let her have one room to herself and I have one room to myself.

Gerry came to the cottage one Sunday afternoon and had a cup of tea. When he started on his "Everything is the Will of Allah", Jinny had a terrific row with him and started throwing crockery at him and anything she could get hold of, and chased him out of the cottage. This suggestion that Allah was responsible for the state of events that we were experiencing got Jinny into a raving temper—if I hadn't have been there, there's no doubt she would have seriously injured him. So Gerry never visited the cottage any more. She was also very unfriendly to Bill when he stopped at the cottage for the weekend.

Christmas 1941 came, but there was very, very little enjoyment anywhere. Nobody was in the Christmas spirit. Jinny said that she was spending her Christmas with her woman friend. So on Boxing Day I went to my usual haunts in Oxford and I met the journalist Hubert Nicholson. His book *Half My Days and Nights*, mentioning me, had just come out. He said that he was living in Banbury and that I should visit him and his wife. This I did and he gave me a copy of the book, which I enjoyed very much. Of course most of the characters who he described in his book, the Bohemian characters, were not the characters of my period of history but were the characters who had congregated around the Coffee An' about two years before the last World War.

I tried bringing Jinny boxes of nice handkerchiefs, pots of honey, chocolates and little bits of presents which I presented to her. But it didn't have any effect at all—she just wasn't interested. When she kissed me in the morning before she went to work she kissed me without any affection at all. She wouldn't caress me and she was as cold as ice. All the affectionate attitudes that she'd had towards me in the past were completely shattered and I often thought to myself, "What have I done to deserve this?" On several occasions Jinny said to me, "You'd better find yourself another woman to love," and I couldn't

Ironfoot in the 1940s.

get her into any serious discussion. Her attitude was: the less she saw of me the better. I experimented on several occasions trying to harmonize with her, but she was very obstinate and she completely disregarded me. Never mind all this nonsense about "It's the Will of Allah"—you can forget that. If all the nonsense I have had to put up with is the "Will of Allah" I'd like to meet this "Allah" and give him some of my ideas on life and the way things *should* be organised.

Anyway, then we had a letter from one of Jinny's girl friends in London. She said the air raids were very bad and, being kept up all day and all night, she was getting worn out. We wrote back and said to come and stay with us. So the following week she arrived and she was quite all right and pleased to see me and pleased to see Bill. She had a Bohemian temperament because she was married to a very unsuccessful song-writer and got her living for years as a waitress in various different establishments where the Bohemians went—the last time we saw her she was a waitress in the Coffee An'. Her husband was in the Forces. Unfortunately she also discovered the unwelcome and the morbid attitude that Jinny was in. She stopped with us for about six months and she got a job in Oxford in a milk bar but Jinny would never go to Oxford with her and never go to the pictures or to any enjoyment. Then this girl got a letter to say that her mother's house in Holborn had been bombed to the ground and had lost everything. So she went back to London to get somewhere for her mother to live. Jinny and me went to the railway station to see her off but we heard no more of her after that.

On his regular visits Bill explained how serious it was getting in London, and eventually one morning I got a letter from the Radcliffe Hospital to say that Bill was in there. I dashed round to see him and he looked very white and pale and had been brought in after an air raid. Fortunately he was only in the hospital for a week and then he came and stopped with us in the cottage for a while. Eventually he found somebody who let him a little houseboat somewhere between Oxford and Abingdon, and started getting his living by buying and selling clutter.

Then we met a little fellow who was for many years a dealer in clutter in the Caledonian Market. He was a little bit disabled in one arm and had lived somewhere round Deptford Broadway with his brother and his sister before they'd been bombed out. His brother had been killed and his sister had gone to live with someone else. So he stopped a couple of nights with us in the cottage and after he'd had a rest he decided to go into partnership with somebody who had a clutter shop in Walton Street, Oxford.

Jinny received some letters from London saying that some of her friends in the wardrobe profession had been bombed out and killed—this didn't make her any better, and I got letters from different friends in London telling me of characters who had been killed in air raids.

Charlie Burns, the Hyde Park orator, wrote me a letter. He was fire-watching in the Underground at Camden Town and he said that he'd had some very narrow scrapes. I wrote back telling him he should come to Oxford for a bit and he did. He was very shaky and nervous. On several occasions I took him to the Ashmolean Museum but the war had caused him to lose the enthusiasm he had had for the subjects he'd been interested in. He took the attitude that he couldn't care less about anything. Then one night, about two o'clock, there was a knock on the door. I thought an air raid had started and we hadn't heard the warning, but this was not so. When I opened the door, there was Walters, the all-in wrestler. He'd arrived on a motor bike and, hearing that I lived locally, decided to come and see me. He explained that he was a Fire Guard in the City and, after staying the night, he jumped on his bike and went back to London.

Then jumble sales started opening in Oxford and in different villages, in Reading and Aylesbury and High Wycombe, and Bill and I went to these sales and bought things that we could sell again at a little profit. The other Bill and this little fellow with the junk shop in Walton Street and my Bill, all used to get together in this little cafe in St. Ebbe's which was called "The Coffee House." It was only very tiny—the room that we met in would hold about fifteen people. But the woman who was running The Coffee House at that time was very interested in Spiritualism and liked me very much because I could talk to her about the Occult. At this period of my life I'd got to a frame of mind where I had no desire to shatter anybody's beliefs. I was convinced of what I believed in. And there was one or two Spiritualists meetings which I went to and, whilst there, I took an attitude of complete passive resistance so far as talking was concerned: I didn't say a word. I went to all kinds of meetings and all I said was "Good evening," when I went in and "good night," when I went out!

We carried on, and Bill was getting a comfortable living with clutter and antiques, and our little friend in Walton Street with a clutter shop was also getting a comfortable existence. Our other friend Bill had a pension from the Navy so he left The Mitre, and he managed to find a cellar somewhere in

Oxford which he turned into a bit of a studio. He also got a part-time job for about two hours in some college washing-up dishes, and he took up fishing and painting in his studio in water-colours. He was no good at portraits but he was very good at water-colour landscapes.

Jinny did not change her attitude, and I couldn't get her to talk about anything and couldn't get her to explain what was the matter. She looked as if she was in a daze, and the happiness had been completely shattered out of her life. I didn't get sentimental and I didn't put it down to the "Will of Allah", but I put it down to the Evolution of the Cause Of Events—there's no doubt that the war was the cause of the unfortunate mental illness which she was experiencing. It was certainly nothing to do with the "Will of Allah" or the will of anybody else—there was a cause, a material cause for it. Then this local woman she had made friends with, and who had got her work in the car factory, evaporated into the elements—she died, and Jinny had lost the only friend she'd made in Oxford. But she managed to get friendly with a few of the London evacuees who were in the village at Headington—Oxford, at this point, was packed to suffocation with evacuees.

One afternoon when I was sitting in the café in the market-place in Oxford, Gerry came in and said, "There are two characters looking for you, and I've told them where you are." And about a quarter of an hour later who should turn up but Gipsy Larry, and with him there was another busker by the name of Australian Jack. Jack played guitar and he'd been playing around Soho with Gipsy Larry and his banjo and some of the other characters. Well, we spent a day or two together walking around the countryside and we took a bus to The Last Chance roadhouse where we stopped all day and came back on a lorry at about twelve o'clock. Larry and his wife had a caravan at Bedford and Larry was working a clutter stall in Bedford Market, and Australian Jack was in the Fire Service in London.

A character who called himself "The Dianotto"—there were other Astrologers in the past who had called themselves this name—came to Oxford with an Astrology board which you work by getting the dates of somebody's birth and you pull the reading out of a slot. He managed to get a barn, for him and his wife to live in, somewhere around Cowley, and he got his living by going to the country markets. He went to Banbury and to Stratford-upon-Avon, and he was in our company for the rest of the war. Bill and I went to Stratford about once a month, and I made friends with Wiggingtons who were the biggest antique dealers in Stratford-upon-Avon. They were charming characters and they were always willing to buy from me but they weren't interested in clutter, they were only interested in genuine antiques.

And then I bumped into a girl I'd known for some years, by the name of Connie, who used to work with an Australian called Frank. I met her as I was walking down Oxford High Street. She told me that Frank had died and that she was on her way to Birmingham. She gave me the address of the people she was going to stay with. We went and had a cup of tea and she seemed very distraught. She was one of the cleverest second-sight workers on the road and I'd had many a chat with her and Frank at different market-places where they'd do a second-sight act. In their spare time they used to visit the Bohemian dives. I walked with her to the railway station and felt very, very sad when I bade her goodbye. Jinny was very upset when I told her that Frank had evaporated into the elements but I had to tell her because Connie had wanted her to write to the address she had given me.

Finally Peace was declared[55] and Jinny packed up her job and went to stay with one of her lady friends in London. Bill went to London too. So I took my sleeping-bag, locked up the cottage and had a week hitching on lorries and in cars. I hitch-hiked right up to Rhyl in North Wales. During that time I was always thinking about what my next move would be. I jumped around from Wales to Hereford, then Worcester and Stratford-upon-Avon. On my travels I found two nice books: one bound in black leather and the other full of colour prints. These I sold in Oxford for twenty pounds.

And the following week I got a letter from Birmingham saying that a character was coming to see me at the weekend with his wife. In his early days he had obtained his living at carnivals on the Isle of Wight, and he and his wife used to seek Jinny's and my company when they were on the Island and he often used to visit us when we were in London at our studio in Hampstead Road. So he came to see us the following week and we had a long discussion, and he said that he had a friend in Birmingham who had the authority to rent an empty house next door to him, both the houses belonging to the same landlady. Jinny went up to Birmingham and stopped at their place for a week and had a look at the house which she liked very much. It wasn't big: it had two little rooms at the top of the house, one moderate-sized room in the front and one moderate-sized room above that, with a kitchen, scullery, tiny cellar and garden.

55 May 8, 1945.

The rent was thirty shillings a week with rates on top. So then I went to Birmingham and had a look at this house, and it was in Handsworth, in the suburbs. Jinny didn't want to go back to London but I could always go back with my sleeping-bag if I wanted to. As a matter of fact Jinny didn't care if I went back for one month or two months or three months; she was still in this peculiar mood.

We decided to take this house. We paid three month's rent in advance and we arranged for a van to collect our belongings from the cottage in Oxford. London Bill had already departed and got himself a shop at the end of Church Street, Edgware Road, buying and selling pictures and prints. The little antique dealer decided to remain in Oxford as did the other Bill. We said our good-byes and we moved into this house in Birmingham. I was quite pleased about the situation because I had friends in Stratford-upon-Avon which was only an hour's ride from Birmingham.

I have not mentioned the names of some of my characters in *The Surrender of Silence* because many of them, although they've led a Bohemian life in their early days through economics and through the change of events, they are probably now leading orthodox and conventional lives, and they're working somewhere and they probably have got themselves homes and new sets of friends. Therefore I consider it wouldn't be fair for me to scream to the world their names and let their friends and their acquaintances know how they solved the problem of existence in the early part of their lives. If any of them read this book I, with all my sincerity, send them my compliments.

BIRMINGHAM

We'd been in the house in Birmingham a month when complete Peace was declared.[56] They dropped an atom bomb on Japan and that was the finish of the War. Everybody was delighted and excited, there were parties in the street, and most people chloroformed their mental apparatus with alcohol. It brought a slight smile to Jinny's face; she became more sociable but still not affectionate. We celebrated with wine and friends; we both got paralytic drunk and went on rejoicing until about four o'clock in the morning.

Jinny had made one room of our house into a modern drawing-room and in the other I constructed my studio and fixed up a little workshop. She put a card in the window, and got two girls in as lodgers. They were usherettes at a local cinema.

Now talking about the cinema: I seldom go myself but when I do it's got to be a historical film. I was never interested in imaginary novels. I like a historical novel which portrays reality, and I think that to see a good historical film portraying some particular epoch of history is a good education because it shows how our forefathers solved the problem and, through

56 August 14, 1945.

their activities, how they have been responsible in producing the situation which this generation is born into. And this generation which is existing now should realize that they are either consciously or unconsciously producing the situation which the next generation will be brought into. So the existing generation today can't be held responsible for a situation which has been created by their forefathers, but they are responsible for the situation which they are creating now for the future generation to be born into. And the underlying motive shouldn't be so much the terrific striving to accumulate wealth, but to build and organize and construct a happier state of affairs for the next generation to arrive into. So the memory of all great reformers who have done something for the benefit of humanity, in some way or the other, should be remembered with reverence.

Anyhow…with my fiddling, and the money from these two girls, we could find the rent and rates without much trouble. I ran around Birmingham and I managed to get some sheet lead and started manufacturing the reproduction medallions of Shakespeare, Napoleon and George Washington. I combed all the clutter shops for little picture frames, and these were costing me about sixpence apiece. I visited all the salerooms of Birmingham, and Wolverhampton and I also went to Stratford-upon-Avon and Leamington Spa, and I managed to get a comfortable living selling my lead pictures. I started using the Kardomah Café in New Street, Birmingham because downstairs, in the morning, the jewellers and the diamond dealers and the antique dealers went down there to talk about deals. I got very friendly with a lot of characters who painted and were interested in literature, and I also made a few friends from the Birmingham colleges.

Jinny didn't want me around her a lot, she seemed to be far happier when I wasn't there. I got a wireless set and she constructed a very nice drawing-room out of second-hand furniture—a settee and arm chairs and carpets, an antique clock on the mantelpiece, and nice cretonne curtains on the window. I hung blackout curtains all around the walls of my studio and I put about a dozen various Oriental large brass trays around. In one corner I had a nice little shrine with a beautiful Buddha on it and an incense burner and joss sticks and all my books.

I went down to London for two days once a fortnight to see what I could see, and had a walk round the West End. There were new cafés opening with new proprietors and there were milk bars opening, and the only truly Bohemian café that was left was "The 91" in Charlotte Street. It would hold about thirty people comfortably. The ground floor was a Greek café and downstairs was used for the artistic people. The proprietor was very friendly towards the Bohemians and I used to go down there and managed to contact a few old-timers. I had a walk around Charlotte Street and I met Boris, who has been in the West End for many years, and was a partner in the Coffee An'. He had opened a night club which he called "The Mandrake Club" and he was very nice to me and said I could come down there any time I liked. So when I was in London I used 91 Charlotte Street, in the basement, and the Mandrake Club. (After twelve o'clock at night there were no cafés open at all!)

There were very few buskers about and I kept on hearing about different characters that had been killed in the war and killed in the air raids, and Boris managed to round up most of the characters that were left, which I should think only consisted of about thirty, and we had a big celebration to open the Mandrake Club.

I carried on the best way I could, and at the end of that September[57] I made a recording for a wireless programme which allowed a lot of people, who knew me all over Britain, to know that I'd survived the War.

Then the next August I had a detrimental vibration. I was sitting in the Kardomah Café talking to two characters and handling hundreds of pounds worth of diamonds which I was going to get valued. However, somebody squealed, and I only had the diamonds in my possession about twenty minutes when squad cars arrived and I was arrested. I went for trial at the Birmingham Sessions and Scotland Yard laid all the details before the jury. I defended myself in the dock the best way I could. In the circumstances I was quite satisfied, because I was not charged with buying stolen property—because I hadn't bought them, I didn't have the money to buy them, anyway—I was charged with being in possession of stolen jewellery knowing it to have been stolen. I straightened this out in the court by proving that I wasn't definitely aware that it was stolen. The diamonds were in two rings and the shanks of the rings were not gold but platinum, which was not marked. They were amongst a lot of theatrical jewellery, in a tin box, which was mostly junk. I was looking at them for some characters who wanted to know their value for which information I was going to get a little commission.

This was in September and I got eight months in prison. I was sent from Birmingham to Reading, and I got a letter from Jinny which put my mind at rest because she said she wasn't worried and she told me not to worry about anything. This prison in Reading was where Oscar Wilde served his sentence and it was

57 I presume 1945.

rather like a fortress. It had been, in years gone by, a monastery, and when I was walking around the exercise ground I did get a feeling like I was in a monastery. I contented myself here. It didn't worry me a lot because it was at the end of the summer and it only meant that I would be in gaol till the spring.

I was put in the woodshed chopping up wood. The smell of the wood, and the view out of the window onto a very nice flower garden, just made me feel that I was near Nature again.

I'm a Buddhist so I asked the Padre if I could send for my books on Buddhism and the *Buddhist Journal* which came out once a month. I also asked the Padre if I could read Gibbon's *History of the Decline and Fall of the Roman Empire*, which he very kindly arranged for me to have sent in from the Public Library in Reading, and I kept these three thick volumes in my cell about three months.

When you're in a place like this, if you have the capability to think, the main thing you do is to try and scheme and arrange some particular type of a plan for your future life when you are free. There were several interesting lectures given, and there was a cinema show once a month and a concert so, taking it all round, I contented myself and took an attitude of complete indifference to everybody. I was sociable, but I kept myself to myself. At this time the prison cells were not lit up with electric light but by gas. There was a table up against the wall and a glass window behind which there was a gas bracket. So when it was lit it didn't completely light the cell but it threw the light right onto my books. The food was plain but in abundance—I was never hungry. And everybody was sociable—even the warders would occasionally smile and the Chief Officers too. The Governor of the prison was very, very sympathetic towards the prisoners, and there was a terrific large exercise ground surrounded, at the back end of the autumn and at the beginning of the spring, with beautiful flowers. Jinny paid me one visit and wrote me letters when I was due to receive them.

Now the time arrived when I was released, and Jinny met me at Snow Hill in Birmingham in a taxi. I had a rest for a couple of days and started jumping about again, came to London, went to the Mandrake Club and did a couple of turns.

Frith Street, when it got dark, was very poorly lit; it looked like the side of a wharf, like a big warehouse. The underworld cafés seemed to be very busy and underworld life seemed to be in full swing round Rainbow Corner and Piccadilly. There was a friend, who I met in The 91, who was a sculptor, and he had a very large studio in the Caledonian Road, with several basements underneath, and I went up and stopped at his place and slept in my sleeping-bag with about five or six other Bohemian characters on the premises. He was a very, very fine sculptor, and he and some friends were making various weird and fantastic bookends and masks and casting them in plaster of Paris which they were flogging to art and clutter shops. Other times I stopped with another friend who had a small warehouse at the back of Hampstead Road, and there were a few Bohemians there who were manufacturing divans. They too all met up at The 91 in Charlotte Street.

Back in Birmingham I had a walk round the Bull Ring and down the Rag Market, and I got friendly with different people with clutter stalls and they were buying my lead sheet pictures.

And there was a fortune teller performing in the Bull Ring with a Mystic Hand, and there was Gipsy Paul with his Astrology board and an Indian selling lucky charms. There were also various kinds of hawkers selling all sorts of novelties and commodities. I had a chat to Gipsy Paul and became very friendly with him; he had been badly disabled in the First World War and walked with a limp. He was living in a mining village about four miles the other side of Handsworth. When I told him I worked in Numerology he said that I could work with him and that he'd take me out to one or two little markets around the Midlands. So that night I went home and made a nice little folding board and composed some readings. I had twelve readings for twelve Numbers. I painted the twelve Numbers on little pieces of cardboard, and I put these into a cigar box. I called this Numerology "Pick Your Number" and went out to one or two places around Birmingham and found that the citizens of these outlying districts were fascinated with my method of Numerology, for which I charged sixpence. On some occasions I went out with Gipsy Paul and we worked what we call "double-handed"—both together—and he was selling an ointment at that time which he called "Hedgehog Fat". He always worked with ear-rings on and a coloured handkerchief round his head.

Then one Saturday we tried the Bull Ring. Now to get a pitch in the Bull Ring in Birmingham it was necessary to be up at six o'clock in the morning, because there was a scramble for pitches. But on Saturday I could get into the Bull Ring at about four o'clock, when some of the other workers had sold out their novelties and there was room to stand my board. Nobody was antagonistic to me over the trouble with those diamonds, and everybody knew I'd been in prison because the *Daily Mirror*, at that period when I was sentenced, had a photograph of me and a short article telling the world that

I was a Numerologist whose Numbers had gone wrong. I did hear afterwards that there was a bit of a controversy with one of the editors of the *Daily Mirror* so I wrote him a letter telling him that his Numbers had gone wrong. As a matter of fact, this publicity of getting myself into gaol over the diamonds made a lot of people more curious about my method of Chance.

I met another character at this time. He was from Coventry and he worked under the name of "Professor Romanoff"—he became a great friend of mine, and we went about together quite a lot when Gipsy Paul was away in other villages. Romanoff considered himself a clairvoyant and he gave readings from his own intuition and sold lucky charms. He was a very handsome fellow and was very interested in history, mostly ecclesiastical history, particularly Martin Luther. He was in possession of a car, which was a great asset to us in running about the Midlands. Well, when we were together in the markets we worked "double-handed" and we shared half of what we took. We went all over the place and we also had a run in the car to Cardiff and Swansea, and we worked one or two other fairs in Wales. We had a beautiful trip, for a week, in the Wye Valley, and we had another trip round through Chepstow and back to Birmingham through Stratford-upon-Avon where we had a chat to Wiggingtons. Romanoff was a convinced Christian, he sincerely believed in a Divine Power and that everything, no matter what, was Destiny which, so far as I was concerned, being a Buddhist, I could never accept. However, we mostly kept our religious opinions to ourselves and never got into any serious discussions or controversies. His lucky charm was a Hebrew charm in brass, it was a little tiny "Magan David"—Shield of David.

Towards the end of that year, Jinny seemed much better. She became very sociable and very kind to me and Bill and the Professor. She made many friends among the neighbours and they were always in and out of the house having a chat with her. I had been in and out of the King's Hall Market in Birmingham and the proprietor asked me whether I would like to be Father Christmas on a wage and a small commission. I decided I would and I got myself a Father Christmas beard and a wig and a gown. Around the inside of this market there was a balcony; you went upstairs and when you got up to the top there were stalls all around and a nice café at the end. I constructed a shrine with holly and mistletoe leaves, a shrine for me to sit in as Father Christmas. I started six weeks before Christmas and I was Father Christmas right up to Christmas Eve. I loved the children, and when they came up to me I said, "You've been looking for me and you've found me at last". There were also a lot of poor Birmingham dead-end kids who used to come and had no money. So I bought a pound's worth of the cheapest little toys and novelties I could possibly find, and when these dead-end kids came up I gave them some little trinket, or a little charm or something, free of charge, and I said, "This is on behalf of Father Christmas". A lot of money was taken; the dips were from a shilling to two shillings each.

Jinny came up to see me performing this Father Christmas business and all my friends came too; and all the people who knew me in the Kardomah Café came as well as some of the market workers in the Bull Ring. There was a little wooden shed on the balcony and a photographer came up there, and he took photographs of me with children sitting on my knee. The *Birmingham Mail* got hold of it and gave me a very nice write-up.

I think the title of the article was 'The Father Christmas who had Played Many Parts'.

When that came to an end I had a little bit of money. The lady who owned our house came to see us from Cornwall and told us she was thinking about selling the property. I didn't say anything to Jinny because I didn't want to put any worry on her shoulders. So I went and bought myself a very nice gipsy caravan for fifty pounds. It could be drawn by a pony but had low wheels and rubber tyres so it could be trailed anywhere by lorry. I put a new mattress in it, plenty of blankets and a couple of bedspreads, and I kept it right out in the open country on a farmer's field which only cost me a couple of shillings a week. I'm still in possession of it and occasionally go to it, and I can shift it anywhere I like by having it trailed to another spot by a lorry but I don't permanently live in it. Jinny didn't know anything about this.

Anyway, I was quite contented because I'd accomplished the feat of having a shelter of my own for the rest of my life.

That autumn, while I was out one morning, Jinny had a fit, and the neighbours called the doctor. They carted her off to the hospital in Birmingham in an ambulance, and she was operated on straight away. I went round to see her that night and Professor Romanoff came with me, and the doctor told me that she'd only got a few weeks to live. The next day they brought her home from the hospital to the house in Handsworth and I sat talking to her. She didn't know that she was going to die and I was warned not to tell her. I looked upon it as a very sad situation, but it was the Evolution of Events by the Forces of Nature and I couldn't do anything about it. She sat up in bed and caressed me and kissed me and then she had a seizure, and she was paralyzed all down one side. All the neighbours and all my friends were very kind to me and very kind to her. I sat up with her all night—and six days later, at about eleven o'clock on a Saturday night, she evaporated into the elements.

I was stunned at the time and Romanoff came and stopped with me at Handsworth. Bill, the Needie dealer, came along and stopped with me, and a lady friend which she'd known for twenty years. That night I wasn't in a mood to remain in my right senses, so I went and got about ten bottles of wine and I went on the wine. They took her away and the funeral was arranged for the following Tuesday. I was in a very funny mood; I wasn't crying and I kept on saying to the neighbours, "It's no use crying. Her eyes are shut, she'll shed no more tears". There was a lot of money spent on flowers. When the respectable Bohemians in Birmingham and the poor workers in the Bull Ring heard about it, an amazing quantity of wreathes and flowers arrived. On the day of the funeral I didn't know much of what was happening because that morning I'd drunk a bottle of wine—however I managed to get through it somehow. I wrote a couple of lines from Omar Khayyam on a piece of paper:

> *One thing is certain and the rest is lies:*
> *The rose that blooms forever, forever dies.*[58]

During the burial, after the parson had given his oration about delivering her Soul to a Divine power, I put a bunch of flowers and this little piece of paper, with the words from Omar Khayyam, on top of the coffin as she was being lowered into the grave—and that is considered amongst some Needies and some gipsies as a

---

58 According to the Edward Fitzgerald translation, the last line of this quatrain (LXIII) reads: "The flower that once has blown for ever dies."

Bohemian funeral...So far as Jinny was concerned, I was glad that the drama was over. And if it's possible for ecclesiastical theories to be correct, either her Soul or her Spirit was floating about the Universe somewhere and, if it had a mind, she would be thinking about me. This was to me only a stimulating theory. However, I wasn't opposed to anybody who believed in this theory. The curtains had fallen on the drama of her life and there's no need for me to say any more about her in my memoirs because there's quite a lot of material about her in *What Rough Beast?*, by Mark Benney. She was buried in a very nice position in the cemetery in Handsworth, and I kept on the wine for a week.

Then I discovered that I couldn't live in the house, so I got my sleeping-bag and arranged to have all the books that I'd collected, over the course of these three years, put in the basement cellar of a lady friend of mine who had a little antique shop in Soho Road, Handsworth. And, three weeks after she'd been buried, I got a letter from the new landlord who said that he'd bought the property and he would give me some money if I would move out. Well...this was right up my street!

Then about five weeks after that I was jumping about in Birmingham and another calamity occurred, the history of which is known only to Scotland Yard. I had another performance in front of the jury at the Birmingham Sessions, after I had had my jaw cracked and been seven weeks in a plastic surgery hospital near Stourbridge (I've actually forgotten the name of the hospital). This is an ordeal I shall always remember because when the porter came in, to wheel me from the ward to the operating-table, I was quite calm and collected, and I said to myself, "This might well be my lot. This is where I might evaporate into the elements". However I woke up in bed after the operation, with two very kind nurses standing each side of me, and after seven weeks I got over that.

There was a bit of controversy between my solicitor, the landlord's solicitor and the Rent Tribunal (who was representing some of the tenants that were in the house), so I went to court. There were big arguments and big discussions and I was very pleased when this ordeal was over.

I received a little bit of money as compensation for evacuating myself, and that night I spent about five pounds treating different market workers, who were friends of mine, to drinks, and then I took the train to Edinburgh with my sleeping-bag.

RETURN TO LONDON: LONDON &
BOHEMIA TODAY

I stopped in Scotland for three months with my sleeping-bag. It was summertime. I didn't need to put myself out to fiddle much because I had quite a few pounds. So I visited Glasgow and walked around Renfrew Street, Argyle Street and the Salt Market but I did not go and see any of Jinny's relations. It had been too far for any of them to come to the funeral in Birmingham, but they had all sent me beautiful letters. I went on to Edinburgh and had a look at the sights. I found some Needies who were settled in the Grass Market and I stopped with them for four days. I went to Dundee and had a walk round the market and I found some Needies there too, getting their living from totting—buying rags and metal. I stopped with them for a couple of days and then went on to Aberdeen, the Granite City, and had a walk round the covered-in market, and stopped for a week on the outskirts with some gipsy tinkers. Then I went back to a warehouse in Glasgow and bought some lucky charms before going on to Rothesay and Dunoon. I stood in different places with a card saying "The Luckiest Charm in the World" and sold my charms for tuppence apiece although I didn't give any reading with them because I didn't have my Numerology board with me. This way I was able to earn about three shillings an hour. I found quite a few tinkers in Scotland who could speak a muddled-up Romany language of which a few words consisted of pure Romany and a few of Jogars Polary.

Then I decided to hitch-hike to London. I went from Glasgow to Dumfries on a lorry and from there to Carlisle and onto Penrith, Kendal and Lancaster. I stopped in these towns for a day or two. I stood in the main thoroughfare with my lucky charms and I was not interrupted by the police. Many passers-by saw my sign and bought a charm and some of the people said "God Bless You", and I thought to myself, "Well, if there is a Divine Power it's about time he *did* bless me." It's an amazing thing how experiences and ordeals like this are liable to shatter your opinions and make your mind go from one theory to another. So I came to the conclusion: "Well, let everybody cherish whatever theory they hold. Good luck to 'em." Why should I be interested in trying to analyse the theories that other people cherish? These people that cherish these theories, many of them are nice, kind, simple people who believe in the philosophy of "live and let live" and it was stimulating to them to buy a lucky charm and concentrate their mind on the possibility of luck changing for them. And this subject of luck and charms is a very, very debatable subject. I've heard hours and hours of discussion on this subject amongst scholars of the Occult.

I arrived at Preston and found some Needie dealers who had settled there, and stopped with them for a day. I worked the covered-in market in Preston but didn't want to go over to Blackpool because I didn't want to see that place again. It would only bring back bad memories of trying to get a living in the early days. So I hitch-hiked from Preston to Manchester and found a

Needie gipsy walking round the back streets. I asked her whether I could come and camp with their family in my sleeping-bag, and she said, "Certainly." They were camping a few miles out of Manchester, and I camped with this family for a month. When I came into Manchester I found that the Corn Exchange had been bombed and there was a big patch of ground that had been bombed near the Chambers. Here I started to "ring pitch"— talking to crowds—again. I just talked about anything that was interesting. I talked about the Incas of Peru and the primitive people on the Easter Islands, pointing out that these primitive people, in their simplicity, actually had a Paradise on Earth in comparison to us, who were more or less chained down to a mechanical civilization. I managed to earn, without any trouble, a pound a day selling my charms. I bought ten pounds worth of charms in the warehouse in Manchester. Then I wrote a letter to the farmer where my caravan was and sent him some money. He replied saying that everything was all right.

When I got to Nottingham I found some Needies who had a small caravan, a pony and a tent. They were camping between Elston and Bulwell, just outside of Nottingham. I had a pitch on these two markets with my charms but I couldn't have a pitch in Nottingham, not talking to the crowd. So I did a bit of "gazing" in some of the streets, and I wasn't interfered with by the police. By this method I managed to get hold of ten or fifteen shillings a day.

I then set off to London where I met a friend of mine who had a little antique shop in Drummond Street, Hampstead Road, and he agreed to allow me to camp in my sleeping-bag in one of his rooms above his shop. I frequently went to see Boris in the Mandrake Club, and I had a look around the warehouses in

Houndsditch and bought one or two cheap bits of jewellery—charm bracelets and cheap rings—to fiddle with.

When I was in the Mandrake Club I was introduced to somebody who was connected with *The People*, and went up to see them at their offices. They said they would like to write an article about me and they would call it "Fifty Years on the Fiddle". I agreed to this and they gave me a few pounds, which I was well satisfied with. The article in *The People* came out that next Sunday morning with a photograph of me walking along the street. This brought me into the limelight again, and one or two of the characters of our old Bohemian world got back in touch.

Well I found myself an attic in Stoke Newington, the rent of which was very cheap. I was over seventy years of age and money was getting very tight, and it wasn't getting any easier to earn money, so I decided to apply for my pension. I went down to the Public Assistance and I told them that I was born in Australia and I'd been in this country fifty years, and they said, "What evidence can you get to prove you've been here fifty years?" And luckily I had a conviction. I was sentenced to prison, for seven days, when I was wandering about the country, for travelling in a railway train and not having a ticket. So I went straight to Scotland Yard and saw one of the officials, who was very sociable, and I asked for a copy of my record as I wanted it to try and obtain my pension. He said that unfortunately they could not let me have the record of my various controversies with the law, but that they would see into the matter for me. He took my address and a week afterwards I got a letter from the Public Assistance and they sent me my Pension Book.

Ironfoot "plunder snatching" on Petticoat Lane, late 1950s.

Well, this stimulated me a little bit because I thought that, at any time I wanted, I could draw my caravan nearer to London and live on my pension without paying very much rent. So I made it my business to visit my caravan about once a month and stop there for a night. This enabled me to put a fire on and dry it out a bit as the interior was getting a little damp.

Somehow or other I can't properly settle. I keep on jumping about all over the place on charabancs. I take the Green Line to Windsor, Reading, Redhill and I go to Brighton and Southend. Then I get a bus from outside Southend station, for five shillings, which takes me to Clacton-on-Sea. I've gone up as far as Great Yarmouth. I do this in winter-time as well as in the summer-time; and all my spare money, if I've got any spare money at all, is spent on jumping about on country buses and hitch-hiking. I can't seem to get the upper hand of this restlessness.

I went down to Petticoat Lane. Nowadays, when market workers come from around the country, they can't work in the Lane, like they used to in the old days, because the Lane is restricted to licensed stall-holders. So the only chance they've got is to rent a stall on a bit of bombed out ground at the top of the Lane at Aldgate. And I thought to myself: "Well, I wonder how a clutter stall will do here?" So I thought I'd try my hand at a game that hasn't been worked for at least forty years—"plunder snatching". And here's the secret: you buy a box of foreign coins and you take these to the Jewel Quarter and you get them gilded. You get a few cheap brass rings, a gross of sewing thimbles, some lucky charms and you get boxes of stones out of broken cheap jewellery (all colours) and bits of broken tin, military badges, jewellery with the stones out and medallions. You muddle all this clutter up on a velvet cloth on your stall and it's not long before you've got a crowd round you sorting it out. You keep shouting out that everything on the board is sixpence, "See what you can find!"

Now you don't put the gilded coins on in a large quantity. You put a few on at a time, five or six, and these will sell quite well because there's a lot of people silly enough to think that you're silly enough to accidentally allow a solid gold coin to be on the stall. The people who buy these gold coins, thinking that they've bought a gold coin, they run away as fast as they can. The thimbles go quite well, and the rings and bangles that you have on the stall are children's rings and bangles; the rings will only fit a little girl or a little boy up to about twelve. That's "plunder snatching". But there's a snag to it: you've got to have a bit of money to start you up because you've got to buy the rings, the charms and the thimbles by the gross and there's purchase tax on them. So to work this game you require at the very least ten pounds.

However, I have now got this game organized. But, under the expensive conditions that we live by to-day, it's not possible to rely on it for a living because you lay out a pound to earn ten bob. Now if you earned this ten bob at the rate of ten bob an hour it would pay you, but you don't. I've tried this plunder snatching game for two years down the Lane every Sunday morning. I've taken it out to Brixton, down The Cut, Waterloo, Shepherd's Bush Market and out to East Lane, Walworth. I've also tried it out on one or two country markets, and the most you can earn is about ten bob a day (by the time you've paid for your commodities, the rent on the stall and your travelling expenses).

I've worked on this ground in Petticoat Lane for three years and I've just packed it up and gone back to gazing with my lucky charms and just going out when I feel like it. I used to enjoy the Lane Sunday morning because I used to see a lot of old friends, but that's gone with the wind now.

Since I've packed up the Lane, I've shifted myself from Stoke Newington and got a tiny place to myself where I can live. I've still got my caravan, which I might settle in eventually, and I've also got other places where I can go with my sleeping-bag and stop any time I like. As a matter of fact, apart from the one place where I've got a few odds and ends, I've got altogether five different places where I can shelter myself for the night.

We are now coming near to the end of the drama of *The Surrender of Silence*. There is a French café in Old Compton Street, a very tiny place, which shuts at nine o'clock at night. It's considered, in the daytime, to be the Bohemians' stronghold. I like to visit this café occasionally and the proprietor allows me to sit, if I want, for three or four hours and I meet a few of the faces from the old days. I'm also very popular amongst the younger generation who aspire to understand Literature, Music, Art and Philosophy. One afternoon an art master walked into the café, recognized me from years ago, and asked me to come up to the Art School in Charing Cross Road[59] and pose for his students. So I went up there and I got a booking. It wasn't difficult for me to pose because I've posed on several occasions for artists in different periods of my life and there are oil paintings about somewhere that were painted of me in my younger days.

So far as getting some money to buy food, I can always pop out to the suburbs for a few hours and stand in the main street, or I can walk up and down a market selling my lucky charms.

So I can always get a few shillings that way when I feel like it. Sometimes I stand on Charing Cross Road for a couple of hours at night or the Strand; some Sunday afternoons, if it is fine, I stand where the street artists do their drawings on the pavement round Sir Henry Irving's statue opposite St. Martin's Church. I only charge tuppence for my charms today because, at the least, I'm sure of earning four shillings an hour. I've tried other little capers but they require too much effort to make 'em pay. Between charms and posing at art schools, I am more-or-less contented and can survive without being on the verge of poverty. I will say this: that I thank the makers of the Welfare State who have given people like me, who live a precarious life, a pension at seventy, because it prevents us from becoming tramps. No matter what fiddling game we were at, we could never earn the money to pay for a furnished room

59 St Martin's School of Art, 107–109 Charing Cross Road, which moved in 2011 and is now Foyles Bookshop.

and most lodging-houses are, at the very least, two shillings or a half-a-crown a night and, with my particular temperament, I couldn't live in one of those places. I'd sooner live in a tent in the open country, or become a vagabond with my sleeping-bag. However, the pension has solved the problem. It pays for a shelter and all I have to do is to get money for food. I get plenty of clothes given to me and I have got a very nice collection of cravats and collars, and about twelve books which I cherish. (If anyone wants the books I left in the cellar in Birmingham they can have them, if they are still there, providing they get a note from me.) And I'm not short of company: I've got several people, including Bill and Professor Romanoff, who visit me and I'm not short of the company of beautiful women either— they seem to like my companionship.

The first Soho Festival—from July 10th-16th, 1956—was very exciting. The people who organized it sent for me and asked me if I could do a turn, and I said that I could do a few monologues, and one of my favourite songs—"I Wonder What it Feels Like to be Poor?" I've sung it for years and it's always caused a certain amount of amusement. So they put me on the programme to perform in the open on Golden Square, in Soho.

Here I am on the programme:

> JULY 10TH, 12.20–1.30 P.M.
> *Cockney Songs & Monologues* by Black Larry & Ironfoot Jack.

> JULY 14TH, 12 NOON
> *Monologues & Ballads* by Black Larry & Ironfoot Jack.

Black Larry has been busking in the West End for years. I recited in Golden Square, in front of a mike, to about four thousand people. I did 'The Dying Hobo' and Harry Champion's 'Any Old Iron'. Then I did 'I Wonder…':

> "Oh I wonder what it feels to be poor?
> To have the wolf forever at your door
> Oh there's thousands of poor men who only get
> Five hundred pounds a week, and ten meals a day,
> A life like that I could not endure.
> Oh how my heart aches when I see the shabby boots and
> clothes they wear,
> Only last night after tea
> A millionaire said to me
> 'Oh I wonder what it feels like to be poor?'"

For the next number I sang 'I'm Burlington Bertie': it's a well-known comical number which ends:

> "I sleep in Hyde Park and I rise with the lark,
> They built Piccadilly for me."

Then at the end of the week all the Bohemians that were left in Soho and all the rising Bohemians who were interested in Bohemian philosophy (although, strictly speaking, it's impossible to lead a Bohemian life now you've got the Welfare State), came to a colossal party. And here is a report of the party which was published in the *Soho Weekly* on 20th of July, 1956:

BRASS BANDS – AFRICAN TOM-TOMS: WILDEST PARTY SEEN IN SOHO
(Soho Weekly Reporter)

What a night—such a night—it really was. Three hundred, singing, laughing, living (im)mortals crowded into Old Compton Street parking-lot last Saturday night to blow out the lanterns of the first Soho Fair.

BONFIRE BROUGHT OUT THE BRIGADE

Soho characters, with their guests from Chelsea, Bloomsbury, St. John's Wood and Hampstead launched themselves into Bohemia's wildest of wild, wild parties.

The merry-making was officially declared open by Ironfoot Jack, who this night added the brightest of jewels to his Bohemian crown.

There was Eileen, the ubiquitous Fox, feverishly transforming chaotic chaos into organized chaos, and Twenty-Stone Tiny, who temporarily deserted the Café Bleu to bring the strains of his accordion to the crowded car-park.

Our 'Hot-Gospel' merchant, Billy Kaye, was almost trampled to death whilst sitting in the dirt with two other musicians banging away at African drums. They very nearly succeeded in drowning the din from a rather powerful brass band.

Local tradesmen, too numerous to mention, made gifts of wine, meat, bread and beer, etc. Even an ox was offered—and gratefully refused until next year!

TRUE SPIRIT

Here was the true spirit of Soho. A little trouble here and there—due mainly to gate crashers—which brought the police out in strength. A prematurely lit bonfire which dragged the Brigade out into the night air, but nothing except an occasional cracked head that the 'Bums' could be ashamed of.

"The police were wonderful," said a 'Bum' chief.

"The characters were very good," reported a police spokesman.

So with gaiety and good-will, the first Soho Fair ended about 3 a.m. on Sunday morning.

And we wish them all—characters, guests, beneficent shopkeepers, police and firemen—Many Happy Returns."

I'd like to add a little bit more to this. I also met at the party a lot of characters I hadn't seen for years. I met Walters, the Hyde Park orator on the Freedom of Thought, and I met a little jockey who I'd not seen for years and a lot more people who remembered me from days gone by. I should estimate that there were quite four thousand people all over the place, some trying to get into the party and some trying to get away. I got on top of a taxi and made a speech. I said that "This party was to unite the Bohemians of all countries into a brotherhood and I hoped it would be laying a foundation of everlasting unity amongst the Bohemians, which was a brotherhood of sincerity."

So that was the end of the first Festival of Soho and there will be some considerable time before there's ever another Soho Festival which could be so gay and so lively. I had been featured on the newsreel, in the Pathé Gazette, and one or two other news films and, as I walked through Soho, they announced, "This is the famous Ironfoot Jack". Last year, so far as the Bohemians were concerned, the Soho Festival was a proper flop; the press didn't give it a lot of publicity. I was in the Carnival on the Sunday in one of the carts. But there was no performing in Golden Square and the organizers put a stop to the artists exhibiting their pictures in Soho Square. Somehow or other, through the trouble there had been in the underworld amongst the racing people, there was a lot of people who stopped away.

Timothy Whidborne did a beautiful oil painting of me, and this painting was exhibited for a week during the Festival in Foyles window, right in the centre of Charing Cross Road, where they put their rare books. This assisted me to get a living a little bit better—and I did well with my charms for tuppence—because lots of people were coming up to me asking for my autograph saying that they had seen an oil painting of me in Foyles window. I liked the painting very much because it was done in the Old Masters style.

These days I'm just chugging along and existing comfortably. I don't go short of cups of tea and cups of coffee and cigarettes. The only thing which is regrettable is that the little Bohemians' café, The 91, in Charlotte Street, is now closed down. As I've said before the proprietor was very sympathetic towards Bohemians, so you could sit there for four or five hours and there was always somebody playing a guitar or a mandolin. You could take a loaf down there with you and you could order a bowl of soup, a plate of boiled potatoes and a cup of tea, and you could have what the Needies called "a little banquet". However, the lease has run out, and The 91 is now shut, so there's another Bohemian rendezvous gone with the wind.

Well, where do they go to now? The rising generation of characters who consider themselves Bohemians, and dress according to their temperament, most of whom obtain their living in the Arts in one direction or another, they go into the coffee houses which have opened all over London. There is not a coffee house or a Bohemian café in existence which is large enough for three or four hundred of them to all meet together. It's a pity they haven't got a Bohemian café about the size of one of the rooms of Lyons Corner House, but of course that can only be put down to a dream. But it's nice to know that there are a few coffee houses where you can go and have a chat. Some of them are very tiny, only holding about thirty or forty people at a time, and you don't get many buskers playing guitars in them. Occasionally you get Bohemians who can play a guitar—but nowadays they are not playing a guitar to solve the problem of existence, they're playing to amuse themselves and a small section of the company. It is also nice to see that some of these coffee houses are becoming artistic in their surroundings. Of course, they're nothing like the Bohemian cafés in the old days which displayed tapestries on the wall, and hung velvet curtains but they're beginning to construct the seating accommodation a lot more artistically. And for the last few years these bars have been popping up all over the place: Earl's Court, Kensington, Chelsea and along the Strand. There are four in Hanbury Street, just off Tottenham Court Road—and the characters who use these places always inform one another when there's a new place opening.

There are quite a number of little clubs round about the West End, and there's quite a number of milk bars, but these places are very seldom used by the characters who call themselves Bohemians. The Bohemian life—what some of us used to call the "Bohemian Republic"—is definitely gone with the wind. I can't see any possibility of it developing again. It seems that the Caledonian Market is closed forever. There are hundreds of dealers and clutter shops who have put up a petition to try and get it opened again. And if it did open again I'm sure that a big crowd of characters would pack up their work and start fiddling an existence like I did. Unfortunately though, all the basements and studios round the West End and Bloomsbury are now occupied as little workshops and store rooms, so I am more or less convinced that the Bohemian life we knew in the old days has gone forever. We are now evolving into a different system of society—even the fair grounds are on the downward trend—and you can more or less content yourself that the days that I have had the pleasure of living through have definitely gone. Out of the crowd who remember the old days—out of the thousands that were about in that time—I don't suppose I could mention thirty now...But it's no good me or anybody else regretting that these days are gone because as things *are*, and as you would like things *to be*, are entirely two different matters.

Many people will be wondering whether I have any regrets of living the fantastic life that I've lived, and whether I regret any of the experiences that I've had, or whether if I had my life to live over again I would make any alterations. Well, the only alteration I would like to have made was to have gotten hold of a big dilapidated mansion in the country and turned it into a Bohemian colony, and had one of the rooms for painting, one with a grand piano for composing and another for writing, with enough land for these characters to grow their own vegetables. Maybe a small printing-press where a journal could be printed and distributed, putting forth different ideas, and a very nice library, with every book under the sun in it, where a little group of scholars could research into history and write articles for the journal. But of course this can only remain as one of my dreams.

But I have actually no regrets at all. I get real, sincere affection and real, sincere hospitality everywhere I go. In these days I don't spend a lot of time in Soho—I'm always out of the West End by eleven o'clock at night. I've got many places where they like to see me and where I'm welcomed, and I'm always amazed at the welcome I get from the teen-agers who have heard about me.

Of course, I have written a few articles lately in different journals. The last article I wrote about Bohemians was in the *Intimate Review*[60]—this seemed to please a lot of people; it was in Volume 2, Number 17. This journal sells for a shilling and it's distributed all over the coffee houses in London. Previous to that, in *The Clubman* in August, 1952, I wrote an article about the Bohemian life of the old days the West End.

---

60 Copies of this journal, edited by the poet John Rety (1930–2010), were not deposited with the British Library (they only have one issue: no. 7, 1954). The University of Nottingham have, in their Colin Wilson Collection, volume 2, no. 18. I have been unable to locate any other copies.

This is a poem I wrote in prison in the old days:

Not Understood

Not understood I mar my path through this
uncivilized sphere,
And as the hours and days go by I think, plan and scheme:
Not understood.
The spells of affection momentary which are attained
from
Woman's beauty and the only stimulus of the
impressions
Gained from various personalities often disturbs
human desires.
But very little can be attained when love and affection are
Sold and bought for fame:
Not understood. One must not expect to attain human
hospitality
Without material gain
Because the time and the day does not permit true
hospitality
To flow, leaving one with unsatisfied desire: not
understood.
And as one approaches and mounts a climax very near to
human desire
It is shattered to dust leaving one to mount
The same craving desire again: not understood.
And in one's indifference, enthusiasm, inspired more
and more.
Until it is bewildered by human nature and prolonged

Effort attained, experienced, then forgotten: not
understood.
Yet the pleasures
Attained from constant effort are priceless and
The only reward for the lapse of time
Drifting with uncontrollable chance, bantering with
romance: not understood.
Yet it is better to have loved and lost, than to have never
Loved at all: not understood.

I did not write this poem for the Bohemians. I wrote it for
the orthodox and conventional people, for them to try and
understand the spirit and feeling of poor Bohemians.

I end my memoirs here—*The Surrender of Silence*. I have no
regrets. I wish everybody who reads this book the best of luck,
and I end up by saying, "Thanks for the memories…"

Yours truly,
Ironfoot Jack

Ironfoot Jack, late 1950s. Photographed by K. N. Singe.

APPENDICES

APPENDIX 1
IRONFOOT JACK'S 4 ADVICES

ADVICE NUMBER ONE

This number indicates individuality, action, aggression, self-reliance, creation. The good qualities of this number are leadership, dignity, inventive genius. Everything is undertaken with all power for an exact object.

It is a fiery, temperamental vibration, colourful and dominant. Full of imagination and beauty, it exerts the most powerful influences upon the persons whom it rules.

Those controlled by this vibration possess great beauty of spirit; there is an infinite amount of gentleness and poetry hidden. To accomplish in your life you should study yourself and your surroundings impersonally, and learn exactly where your best chances of success lie.

You are specially gifted for investigation, often a question of seeking novelty; artistic taste is usually present; have outstanding ability for understanding others.

Before making use of your impressions determine in advance if they are practical. Don't attempt to get rid of irritations by ignoring them. Forge ahead to the full extent of your abilities in your course of action and wait the development of events. Develop all plans, so that when ready you can launch them with confidence. Find out the cause of a situation and anticipate the consequences. Become aware of approaching changes.

ADVICE NUMBER TWO

This number indicates organisation work, service and endurance. The good qualities are strength of purpose towards unpleasant jobs, usefulness and deliberation.

This is one of the most stalwart, dependable and honest of all vibrations. Those influenced by it are the salt of the earth. They are the back-bone of the community in which they live.

Born home-makers, who work cheerfully and successfully, fortified by self-respect and the respect of those about them. They are peace-loving and tolerant, but able, if need be, to fight valiantly for their principles.

Strong characters with clearly formed ideas on their ambitions, usually highly competent and abounding in the skill necessary to drive their plans to completion.

Anticipate the consequences of any action. Know the cause of a situation. Be aware of approaching changes and turn these changes into advantages. Don't become fascinated with the wrong person. Develop your own formula. Depend on your own impressions more. Under the circumstances, the safest way to avoid difficulties is not to assume too many responsibilities.

ADVICE NUMBER THREE

This number indicates faithfulness, over-honesty and dependability. The good qualities of this number are undying support and assistance when given to a person or cause.

This is the vibration of great courage. It gives a dominating power and the ability to think and live independently. It is, primarily, the vibration of the pioneer, the inventor, the explorers or anyone who aims at originality in any line.

Your outward character—the impression you make on people, the new opportunities for success, the power to express your hidden desires—can influence others for good.

Curious, alert, they see everything and have an amazing diversity of interests often accompanied by powerful intellectual, as well as physical, powers; enthusiasts.

You don't want to be held responsible for the work or actions of others; the illumination of your ideals let them guide you. Retain your sense of proportion so as not to defeat your purpose. Be sure, however, that what you do is practical. Find out what you can do better. Anticipate the consequences of any action. Become aware of approaching changes. Don't become fascinated with the wrong person under the circumstances. The safest way to avoid difficulties is not to assume too many responsibilities.

ADVICE NUMBER FOUR

This number indicates diplomacy, balance, contrast. The good qualities of this number are a sense of justice, tactfulness, and the desire for peace and association.

This is one of the gentlest, most friendly and peace-loving of all vibrations. Those under its influence are both lovable and are ruled by tact, kindness and conventionality. They are desperately unhappy if they are censured or disliked by those around them, but also quiet and domestic by temperament.

Of this vibration are the arts. Music, the plastic arts, literature, the drama—these are the motivating powers in this talented, sensitive and extremely powerful vibration.

Before making use of your impressions determine in advance if they are practical. Exchange ideas with people who can supply you with interesting facts, but be careful how you make use of information, because the more exciting you are the greater can be your gain. Forge ahead to the full extent of your ability. With determination go ahead steadily in your chosen course of action. Focus your attention on matters at a distance.

APPENDIX 2

'THE DRAMA OF LIFE'
A PAMPHLET BY IRONFOOT JACK

Man comes into the world without his consent and leaves it against his will. On earth he is misunderstood; in infancy he is an angel; in boyhood a devil; in manhood he is considered a fool.

If he has a wife he is tied up for life.

If he is a bachelor he is considered inhuman.

If he enters a public-house he is said to be a drunkard, if he doesn't he is considered to be a miser.

If he is poor they say he has no brains.

If he is rich it is said he has had all the luck in the world.

If he has brains he is considered a citizen.

If he is religious they say he is not interested in this world and if he is not religious they say he is wicked.

If he expresses his individuality and wears a beard or long hair they call him a crank.

If he does not work, he does more work by avoiding it than doing it.

If he reads books he is considered a dreamer.

If he is a Bohemian and he works to live and does not live to work then he is considered an eccentric.

If he wants to alter society he is considered barmy.

If he is broke and tries to make a fortune they say he either lands up in Park Lane or Parkhurst.

If he believes all he is taught he is said to be happy.

If he is a busker they say that the street is his stage.

If he is a tramp they say all that is supposed to matter to him is meaningless words.

If he is a gypsy they say he is a child of the sun; no man's master, no man's slave.

If he gambles with his life they say destiny is either his friend or his foe.

If he is a clown they say he is thinking of the limelight and fame.

If he is a wide boy he is considered smart but dishonest.

If he gives to charity they say it is for advertisement.

If he doesn't he is said to be mean.

If he dies young people say there was a great future for him.

If he lives to a ripe old age everybody hopes he has made a Will.

If he is poor, he is despised; if he is rich he is envied.

If he has done all he can to operate society they put up a statue for him.

If he is an aristocrat, they say that all his problems are solved.

If he is a scholar, they say that he knows what he knows.

If he knows what love is, they say he has lived.

When he comes into the world, everybody wants to kiss him,
Before he goes out everybody wants to kick him.

Iron-foot Jack
Karma Yogi, Occultist.

Celebrated Bohemian, portrait model for artists; writer of articles on Bohemian and Gypsy Life, author of *The Drama of Life*. Painted by Timothy Whidborne, pupil of Pietro Annigoni; this painting was exhibited in Foyles Bookshop front window to the public in 1956. Painted by Louis Monroe miniature artist, and Elizabeth, daughter of the Brazilian Ambassador at Cheyne Walk, Chelsea. Has also been painted by many artists at different Schools of Art. Variety artist—monologues—written about in many books by famous authors.

Try sitting still for one hour without moving. This is called modelling for artists. I have done it for five hours daily, sitting still without moving.

Press Report.

APPENDIX 3:

LETTERS FROM IRONFOOT JACK TO COLIN WILSON

Editor's Note: These letters were mostly written in 1957 although Jack did not date them. Those with precise dates have surviving envelopes with legible postmarks. He completed *The Surrender of Silence* in 1956 and arrangements for it to be typed were made by the artist Timothy Whidborne's secretary. Colin had left London by 1957 and it appears that the manuscript came to him through 'Tom', almost certainly Tom Greenwell, who was a gossip columnist for the *London Evening Standard* and a friend of Colin's, who subsequently rented a room with him, Stuart Holroyd, Bill Hopkins and John Braine in a house on Chepstow Road.[61] Jack's eccentric spelling is challenging. With the reader in mind, I have seen fit to tidy-up his errors.

---

61 See Colin Wilson's 'Introduction' and Stuart Holroyd's 'Afterword' to Tom Greenwell's play *Chepstow Road*, Nottingham: Paupers' Press, 2002.

Chelsea
(no date)

Dear Friend

Last August Timothy Whidborne and his secretary arranged
to have my manuscript typed. Timothy is now in Italy and I
have been looking for his secretary and, at last, have found him
and obtained a written document from him signed 22/8/57
to this effect: Jack may arrange as he sees fit to publish his
Memoirs. There is nothing on this document about who
should publish it. The document from Timothy's secretary
makes me entirely free to handle the situation entirely as I
please. I can even sell it for a song if I want to but I am leaving
the whole situation to you as I know by your kindness of
handling the manuscript I will get more than peanuts. Now my
mind is free thanks to you and Tom who by your letters want to
befriend me sincerely.

Ironfoot Jack.

Chelsea
(no date)

Dear Friend

I'm so glad Tom is sending you *The Surrender of Silence*. I am entirely at your disposal to do whatever you want me to do. I have an enormous amount of material I can tell to a shorthand typist about myself and Bohemians and West End history between the last two world wars. I am also willing to go on TV. I am willing to do all you want me to do as I am hoping for a little more comfort out of life because for the last 8 years I have only been able to earn peanuts. A change would certainly revive my mind. I know that there is only one great force which no one can ever enslave or destroy, and that great force is thought. Thoughts and experience have great effect upon human activity. All I know and all my experience in human activity is at your disposal. I wrote *The Surrender of Silence* under great difficulties being annoyed at fiddling about getting the means of life with no time to study my manuscript properly. I realise, as you say, that there is more work to do on it and am so pleased that Tom has sent it to you.

Week after week I only get enough money to get by with very little extra money to get what I really want. Since the article in *Reynold's News*[62] kind people have sent me honey and cigarettes and I am trying hard to get a new cloak as my one is like a rag store. I am also pleased with Tom's letter to you and all you are doing for me—it brings some sunshine in my life.

62 See Appendix 4.

I can also give you some of my conclusions on tramps by desire and tramps by ambition. Also Bohemians by circumstances, Bohemians by desire and Bohemians by ambition. And more material about fair grounds, night clubs, racing boys, market workers, fiddlers, schemers and dreamers. I also know that *The Surrender of Silence* will be the greatest book ever written on Bohemians in Europe—not fiction but reality; the life I chose to live. It will be a sensation to modern society how the other half lived in those dreamy days gone by and a good lesson to the rising generation. It is a memory of beauty, literature, art, philosophy and plenty of poverty and love. As history never repeats itself it will be a book that will shine like a star and all the Bohemians that have gone with the wind will know that Ironfoot Jack loved them. I have written *The Surrender of Silence* not so much for my material gain but to the memory of a glorious past of Bohemian life which is now gone with the wind leaving behind only memories and a brief spell of passion and strife. To a Bohemian this is what they call life—well, I could laugh and I could cry but I have learned to understand that if things are because they are they cannot be anything else than what they are. So all I can say now is; thanks for the memories.

I am at your disposal to do all the arrangements about *The Surrender of Silence* and thanks for all your kindness and all you are doing for me.

Yours sincerely,
Ironfoot Jack

(no date)

Dear Friend

At Guildford College on Tuesday, School of Photographic
Art. Walked around the town on Monday and was made a
Honorary member of the Spider's Web coffee club, Stoke
Road, Guildford. Did a turn there in wigs—some of my old
numbers and the monologues. They liked 'The Dying Hobo'.
Also collected some pictures of myself as a gipsy and one
in a toga—these you will see when you come up to town.
Many students are reading your book *The Outsider*; you have
inspired them.

Thursday night I am at St Martin's art school and Saturday
morning 2 hours Ealing photo studios, Ealing College. I am
now organised for the winter: bought 2 blankets and 2 old
dressing gowns for props for posing in the art schools. Gave
about 200 pamphlets of my *Drama of Life* away in Guildford.
The Spider's Web is quite artistic with subdued artistic lighting.
I also met a poet who had tramped across France and Italy
bumming his way all the time.

Monday night I stayed at The Royal Arms Hotel on North
Street Guildford. Took my ground sheet with me and put it on
top of the bed, nice and warm. This I always do when I travel
from town to town. Also got another day's work at Guildford
Friday week all day. Got back to Chelsea 11.30 o'clock. Trying
to get some variety bookings for Christmas in night clubs. Met
an old timer—a Needie—selling *Moore's Almanac* round the

pubs about 8 o'clock; gave him two shillings and spoke the Jogars Polary (the Needie's slang) with him.

Hope to get some photos with my wigs on. My American friend sends his regards. At night he is at St Martin's School of Art. Many Bohemians who used to survive by fiddling have had to go to work as they cannot get a living fiddling these days. Also these days it is dangerous not to be working, for somebody under 50 years of age.

I have plenty more material for you.

Yours truly
Ironfoot Jack.

Chelsea
(no date)

Dear Friend

Thanks for your kindness and a lovely talk for fifteen minutes. I am looking forward to spending a few hours when you come up at the end of the month.

The characters which I write about in my days before the last World War, because of the way they dressed and their attitude to life, they could not get work if they wanted it. There were many workers out of work who knew how to work and to get a job in those days. You had to have a reference from where you was last working. Besides they did not want orthodox work as, in those days, they could fiddle, if they knew how, to get enough money for food and shelter from day to day. They were not welcomed in any orthodox cafés and restaurants. Soho and the West End was the only place they were welcomed. Many cafés got a living by catering for these characters only and, in general, the general public steered clear of these places. So all these characters congregated together amongst themselves and found their own Brotherhood. In those days the unemployment for workers who knew how to work was a tragedy. It was useless for these characters, including myself, to try and find work apart from being self-employed: busking, modelling or selling cheap commodities. These characters were only made happy in the West End. Although they lived under society they were not of it. They could not afford to go to amusements so they bought a book in the bookshops outside in Charing Cross Road for 3d or 6p or 1/- and read what appealed to them. They all had their particular authors that they loved. The last World War shattered everything: Bohemian cafés, 5/- a week basements and cellars, camping out on the London commons. Those days are over now; the young authors in the next 20 years will not have any of the material to write about. What I have put in my book is the end of poverty and love and I do not think that situation will develop again. Many characters got killed in air raids and evaporated into the elements, many are in old people's homes and institutes. The teen-agers of today know nothing about those days and I have not found any old timers who are interested in writing about it. Even the gipsies who are left stop in one encampment and do not travel much. Today if you are not working and have no money and are not putting stamps on your card you can get sent to prison. They will find you work when you get out and also assist anybody who is destitute—this is the Welfare State. A few old pavement artists are allowed and a very few old buskers. And you cannot get any shelter for under £1 a week these days whereas before the War you could live very well on 3/- a day.

I will work all this material out and describe each personality (how they looked and talked). I shall give myself 5 days rest somewhere in the country and will think things out better. There is no one else who has got the material that I have got. With rest and without worry about the means of life I can dictate much better.

Yours truly
Ironfoot Jack

[**Probably early September 1957**]

Dear Friend

Bank Holiday Monday took £1 with the *Drama of Life* pamphlet. Then rain all the week. Friday went to Mitcham. Wind blowing…no people on the fairground 8 o'clock at night.

Only 4 old-fashioned roundabouts with old-fashioned pipe organs playing opera which reminded me of the old days. My duplicating bureau is on a fortnight's holiday so no pamphlets on the *Drama of Life* for sixteen days.

Went to Brighton at 5.20 in the early morning from Victoria (4/6d return). Arrived in Brighton about 7 and went to the slum quarter for a breakfast. After having a wash and brush-up left the slum café at 8.30. Walked around second-hand clothes shops in the slums of Brighton looking for a second-hand tapestry waistcoat and a velvet jacket or a black pair of corduroy trousers—couldn't find anything. Then my luck changed and I found a second-hand clothes shop at the top of Church Street. Bought a Victorian black suit for £1. Got it on half-an-hour later and threw my rags into a dustbin. I now look like an old city stock broker. Presentable at last! Bought a yard and a half of silver material and made a new cravat which looks beautiful with my silver cravat ring. Could not find a second-hand opera cloak anywhere though.

Had a walk around Brighton until 4 o'clock in the afternoon and got the 5-something back to Victoria. Arrived back at my studio in Chelsea and had a pint of milk, some cheese spread sandwiches and a tin of sardines. Went to bed at 9 o'clock and slept until 1 o'clock Sunday morning. Writing this letter in the coffee house on Northumberland Avenue, Trafalgar Square.

Yours truly
Ironfoot Jack

Chelsea
14 October 1957

Dear Friend

Events in London in our Bohemian world are becoming
entirely different. History does not repeat itself, it may only
appear to do so. Today we are confronted with the task of
creating a new culture and watching events and our thoughts in
a spirit of creative will towards the future of history. All is based
on outer and inner causes of their effects.

There is no Bohemian café apart from the Maleselo, 32
Percy Street where all types of thinkers can meet and only a
small circle use this. Characters who used to use the West End
at night do not come into town now because there is nowhere
to go. Some characters are trying to open an intellectual
café bar around the British Museum. I have been invited to
cooperate with them and I will do all I can to bring in a new
culture to fit the age we have arrived in. Some journalists
photographed me yesterday on the pitch outside the National
Gallery, Trafalgar Square where I was pamphleteering my
Drama of Life to a crowd of people and they are going to write
an article about the pavement artists and buskers of London
and going to send me a copy which I will send on to you. In
order to get them to buy my *Drama of Life* it is much better if I
talk to them a little first.

Down the Lane [Petticoat Lane] on Sunday morning it was
quiet. This is because the Lane has had its day and new shops
in the suburbs and small towns sell just as cheap as the Lane

and the competition in commodities is terrific. Many stall holders do not rely on it for a living. They work all the week and only come out on a Sunday. I shall leave the Lane out of my activities.

Many characters do not use the French café any more as it has been invaded by sightseers and I am only there for an hour from 8-9 o'clock at night. I am looking forward to re-organising myself as events in human activity are moving so rapidly that solutions for me require deep thought for Balance. The posing for artists at the Art School for me is also out of my activities. This is because it has been invaded by all types of characters who think modelling for artists is a wonderful career. Little do they know that it is only peanuts!

Ironfoot Jack.

APPENDIX 4:

IRONFOOT—LAST OF THE BOHEMIANS
BY JOHN ENNIS

Extracted from *Reynold's News*

OCCULT PHILOSOPHY ON SMALL
CIGARETTES AND POTS OF HONEY

I found the last of the Bohemians sitting in a dark corner of a French coffee bar in Soho, talking confidentially to a couple of acquaintances.

He wore a black homburg hat, a black cape with slits to put the hands through, a black shirt, a white collar, a cerise satin cravat held in place by a heavily embossed silver ring, a black corduroy jacket and brown corduroy trousers.

When I said I should like to talk to him, he said "Let's go somewhere quiet."

HIS STORY

He stood up, picked up a walking stick and a dark blue cloth bag overloaded with second-hand books, dog-eared press cuttings, grimy notebooks and the typed manuscript of his life-story, and he limped through the door.

He limped because his right leg is shorter than

the left by some inches. He refuses to reveal what accident in his youth caused his lameness. To overcome it he wears a surgical boot with an iron extension below the sole.

Sometimes he calls himself Professor J. R. Neave, but mostly he is known as Ironfoot Jack.

We sat in a deserted restaurant. Ironfoot Jack lit a small-sized cigarette and let it bob up and down on his lip as he talked.

"There's a lot of people confused about what a Bohemian really is," he said, "he is a person who loves literature, music, art and philosophy so much that he intends only to work to live, and doesn't intend to live to work. All I have to concern myself about these days is my food and cigarette money and bus fares. I'm 77 now and I get my pension. That pays the rent of my studio. If I earn enough in one day to last me for three days, I don't do anything else until I have conked out of money."

Ironfoot Jack wakes in the morning and does "Yoga relaxing" by stretching his arms and legs as far as possible. He drinks a pint of milk a day and, when he can afford it, eats a pot of honey a week.

He sets out from his home in Chelsea for the West End. There he combs second-hand bookshops for "books on occult philosophy and Yoga wisdom."

PUPILS

These he resells. "I have a circle of pupils who are delighted if I can find the right books for them." He dug into his blue cloth bag and brought out a book.

It was called *The Brotherhood of Light*, and sub-titled the Laws of Mediumship and Occult Data. The book was published in Los Angeles in 1921.

"This is the one I look for most," Ironfoot Jack said.

From the bookstalls he goes to the French coffee bar in Old Compton Street, a haunt of art students from the nearby St. Martin's Art School.

Ironfoot Jack rummaged again in his bag and produced a letter certifying that he had posed for painters at the school and a photograph of a full-length painting of him done by Timothy Whidborne, a pupil of Annigoni.

"I am also a bit of a comedian," he said, "and occasionally I get booked as a guest artist in night clubs. In the winter time I get a lot of bookings with a skiffle group. I sing 'Any Old Iron' and do a monologue called 'The Dying Hobo'. And I sing a comical number entitled 'I Wonder What it Feels Like to be Poor?' It's very humorous satire."

FORECASTS

A few years ago he played Father Christmas in a department store. Until the price of market pitches became too high ("they charge you ten bob where it used to be fourpence") he used to sell sixpenny forecasts based on the science of numerology.

He based his forecast on the street number of his client's home. His method was to add the digits of the number together and, according to the result of this sum, choose one of the 24 different forecasts "composed by myself," which he carried ready typed on small sheets of paper.

I asked how such an arbitrary thing as a street number could influence anybody's life. "This is my own system of numerology," he said, lighting another in a chain of small cigarettes. "It is a psychological coincidence that they get into a house with a certain number, and all numbers carry vibrations."

HAPPY LIFE

"I don't give them a dynamic reading. It's a theoretical and abstract speculation. Each forecast begins with the words 'It is possible.' If it didn't have that on I could be pinched for fortune telling."

Though Ironfoot has spent most of his life scraping a Bohemian living, he has been up as well as down.

"I have had a romantic and happy life," he said. "I've been a tramp, I've been in the workhouse and I've been in prison. I've slept at the Royal Hotel and the Grand Hotel, and in hotels at spas. I've run a theatrical boarding house, two Bohemian cafés, three night clubs, a school of wisdom and Children of the Sun, a materialistic religious group. At one period I could write a cheque for £9,000."

MOON TEMPLE

The clubs he ran always had a background of the occult. His term in prison followed a police raid on one of them in the 1930s when policemen were shocked by the antics of some of the Bohemian members.

His last organisation, the Temple of the Moon, is typical of most of the clubs he ran. Ironfoot Jack described it to me: "The philosophy of the Temple of the Moon was that when you die you become part of the elements. Your soul goes to the moon and your intelligence goes to the sun. This theory was put forward, not by me, but by a white Yogi. We had rituals and pagoda dancers. I gave a sermon and I evoked beneficial vibrations and disbanded detrimental ones. Nothing to do with black magic. I have always been opposed to black magic. It's of no asset to humanity at all. The Temple collapsed when the war broke out."

Ironfoot took his last cigarette from the packet.

"At one time I used to visit the British Museum once a week. These days, when I have the money, I enjoy charabanc rides on Sundays to Brighton or Southend. That's my only enjoyment outside of Soho—charabanc rides."

He began stuffing his papers and books back into his cloth bag. "I'm not advising anybody to become Bohemians," he said. "It's not so rosy as it's supposed to be, once you have trained yourself to getting a wage packet every week."

TATTOOED

He shrugged his cloak around his shoulders, preparing to leave. He reached out a tattooed arm and poked thoughtfully among the debris in the ashtray. He hesitated a moment, then his fingers idly picked out the ends of the cigarettes he had smoked.

And Ironfoot Jack stumped out, back to his corner in the French coffee bar, to talk to his friends about literature, art, music and philosophy, and perhaps Yoga, or perhaps only to hear the latest gossip drifting in from the Charing Cross Road.

INDEX

STRANGE ATTRACTOR PRESS

2018